CAN YOU SEE
GOD
IN NATURE

WILLIAM T. SMITH

ISBN 979-8-88945-012-2 (softcover)
ISBN 979-8-88945-013-9 (ebook)

Printed in the United States of America.

Brilliant Books Literary
137 Forest Park Lane Thomasville
North Carolina 27360 USA

CONTENTS

BOOK THREE

BOOK FOUR

BOOK FIVE

BOOK SIX

BOOK SEVEN

BOOK EIGHT

BOOK NINE

MY THANKS

In every poem and thought I wish to thank my Lord, Jesus.
Also, to my family and friends, who some of these are about.
I also want to thank my grandchildren, a joy in to my heart.
A special thanks to my brother Jim, whose book
"Nuggets of Gold" ISBN 978-0-692-06545-7.
A special thanks to my nephew Herbie, whose book
"Keepers of Dawn" E-book only.
They keep inspiring me to write, and live for Jesus.
A special thanks to the soldiers who keep us free.
A special thanks to the ministers who preach God's word.
A special thanks to the doctors and nurses around the world.
My thanks and prayers be with you all—Amen.

William T. Smith

THE DEDICATION

I wish to dedicate this book to my grandchildren Trevor and Austin

A NOTE FROM THE AUTHOR

I wish to thank my Lord and Savior for this book.
It was Him that laid a book on my heart to write.
These poems and thoughts are to honor and glorify my Jesus.
I may have penned them, but with the HELP of the Holy Spirit.
For the Holy Spirit wrote them on my heart, to give unto you.
My prayer is that these poems and thoughts will somehow inspire you to write.
Please let Jesus into your heart, that way you also can write about Jesus.
Thanks very much for everything now and in the future.

William T. Smith

Permission from Memorial Home Hospice:

These poems and thoughts, and parables came from my life experiences:

The Holy Bible K. J. V.:

Things I have read in newspapers:

Things I heard on TV. And Internet news:

Explore the Bible/Lifeway:

To best of my knowledge, I have not copied from anyone.

William T. Smith

BORN AGAIN

Have you ever wondered what the phrase "born again" means? The Bible records that Jesus used the Phrase in a conversation with a man named Nicodemus. Nicodemus approached Jesus at night. He was curious about Jesus and the kingdom of God.

Jesus told him: "Unless someone is born again, he cannot see the kingdom of God" (John 3:3). Nicodemus responded, "But how can anyone be born when he is old?" (John 3:4).

Nicodemus was a highly moral man who obeyed God's law. He was a respected leader of the Jewish community. No doubt he was a fine man. Yet something was lacking. Like Nicodemus, many people today confuse religion with a new birth in Christ. Phrases like "I believe there is a God" often are confused with a real new-birth experience.

New birth begins with the Holy Spirit convicting a person who is a sinner. Because of sin, we are spiritually dead. For this reason, spiritual birth, as Jesus described it, is necessary. God loves us and gives spiritual birth when we ask Him for it.

The Bible says all people are sinners (Romans 3:23). Jesus died on the cross and was raised from the dead to save sinners, to be born again means that a person admits to God that he or she is a sinner and repents of (turn from) sin, believes in or trust Christ, and confesses faith in Christ as Savior and Lord. Jesus told Nicodemus that everyone who believes in (places faith in) Christ would not perish (John 3:16). Jesus is the only One who can save us (John 14:6).

Jesus Christ was with God the Father before the world was created. He became human and lived among humanity as Jesus of Nazareth. He came to show us what God the Father is like. He lived a sinless life, showing us how to live; and He died upon the cross to pay for our sins. God raised Him (Jesus) from the dead.

Jesus is the source of eternal life. Jesus wants to be the doorway to a new life for you. In the Bible, He was called the "Lamb of God" (John 1:29). In the Old Testament, sacrifices were made for the sins of the people. Jesus became the sacrificial lamb offered for your sin.

Jesus said, "I am the way, the truth, and the life. No one comes to the Father except through Me" (John 14:6). He is waiting for you now.

* Admit to God that you are a sinner, means to repent, or turn away from your sin.

* By faith, receive Jesus Christ as God's Son and accept Jesus' gift of forgiveness from sin. He took the penalty for your sin by dying on the cross.

* Confess your faith in Jesus Christ as Savior and Lord.

To believe in Jesus is to be born again. Confess your sins and ask Jesus right now to save you. "Whoever calls on the name of the Lord will be saved" (Acts 2:21).

You may say a prayer similar to this as you call on God to save you: You must do this with an honest, willing heart.

"Dear God, I know that you love me. I confess my sin and need for salvation. I turn away from my sin and place my faith in Jesus as my Savior and Lord. In Jesus' name I pray, Amen".

After you have received Jesus Christ in your life, tell a pastor or another Christian you have received Jesus Christ in your life, share your decision with another person, and following Christ's example, ask for baptism by immersion in your local church as a public expression of your faith (Romans 6:4; Colossians 2:6).

EXPLORE THE BIBLE
Lifeway

PLEDGE TO THE AMERICAN FLAG

I pledge allegiance to the flag of the United States of America, and to the republic for which it stands.
One nation under God, indivisible, with liberty and justice for all.

PLEDGE TO THE CHRISTIAN FLAG

I pledge allegiance to the Christian Flag and to the Savior for whose kingdom it stands.
One Savior was crucified cameming again with life and liberty to all who believe.

PLEDGE TO THE BIBLE

I pledge allegiance to the Bible, God's Holy Word, I will make it a lamp unto my feet and a light unto my path and will hide its words in my heart that I, might not sin against God.

Book
ONE

THE BOOK I WROTE

My name is William T. Smith, a faith poet, and author.
I wish to share with you, my thoughts on nature.
And: My thoughts on our Lord and Savior (Christ Jesus).
What you will find is this; He (Jesus) is always with us.
Some of these thoughts most certainly make you laugh.
And laughter is a very good healer, as we all know is true.
Some of these thoughts will absolutely make you cry for sure.
While others' thoughts will surely make you ask why, with a sigh.
There is a message in all of these thoughts about God, of course.
As you read them, I hope you will be able to think and write yours.
When you read what I have, I hope that you will do better.
Try it, and see what happens with E-mails or in your letters.
One thing I wish you to know; I have a relationship with Christ.
Jesus is my friend, my financial adviser, the only one I trust.
I wish you to meet this savior of mine; my Lord and King.
Will you please call on him, in good times or in times of need?
You may call him God - Lord - Jesus - Brother - or Friend.
When I die, I would very much like to meet with you in Heaven.
My prayer is that you will get a copy and start reading it today.
Tell me what you think about what's written, and what I have to say.
Hope to see you on a bookstore shelf, or maybe in the library.
You may not get rich, but the fact is this: You will not be sorry.

William T. Smith

SEE GOD IN NATURE

There is an old saying, as I have been told.
Through nature, you can see the Lord.
As I look all around me, sitting on the porch.
Nature, in all its splendor, gleams like a torch.
In the winter, everything looks as dead.
Just as we are without Jesus as our head.
Then comes spring and everything becomes alive.
This all comes from the beginning with the light.
As you see, the people and animals giving birth.
Then you know life is great here on this earth.
When you see the wind blowing through the trees.
And watching the birds fly in the breeze.
None of this is by accident or from evolution.
But the little and the big are all God's creation
.

William T. Smith

TRUE LOVE

What is this thing we call "true love"?
True love is simple when it excels above.
So how can I excel in this situation?
I see that trouble starts within a relation.
Seldom will your spouse be perfect.
You must look over the things they lack.
When you do, you are putting love above.
You irritate me. We must work it out in love.
That is true love, be it spouse, child, or parent.
Overlook the small, and focus on the person.
This cannot be done without wanting true love.
You get this kind of love only from God above.
Repent and ask Jesus to come into your heart.
The true love of Jesus will never be apart.

William T. Smith

BLOOD BROTHER

The American Indians has a custom within all tribes.
Their tribe can travel throughout where they abide.
A stranger can make friends and be part of that tribe.
But he must go through a ceremony of that tribe.
A simple ceremony, that they must do in this matter.
Take a knife and slice their wrist on the right arm.
Then they clasp their arms together, so the blood intermingles.
They make a covenant with each other as the tribe watches.
The stranger is now been adopted into this peculiar tribe.
Everything the tribe has is now available to him.
No matter what happens, he will always be the chief's son.
He can never be cast aside, for he and the tribe are one.
Jesus did this same thing, when he chose to die on the cross.
His blood washes away the sin we committed while being lost.
You let Jesus know that you wish him to be your LORD.
He will forgive your sin, and with Jesus you will abide.
Jesus becomes your blood brother in the spirit.
Everything in heaven, becomes yours to inherit.
For where Jesus is, you will also forever be.
For you will walk with him, his peace you will see.

William T. Smith

A CRITICIZING PERSON

You may know this person; you may know him or her very well.
It may be the person at your work, or the one you're married to.
This person is really not that bad, or really mean at all.
The way they were raised, determines what they were taught.
This person that I'm talking about is just simply this.
They are critical of everything, and just need to bitch.
This person will always want you to think the way they do.
And when you finally do think that way, they are mad at you.
I cannot hate this person: this is the way they were raised.
All I can do is witness to them, and give Jesus all the praise.
I must do this every time I am criticized or put down.
I know one day they will accept Jesus as Lord, and be sound.
Jesus is the way into their heart so that they will stop criticizing.
Once Jesus comes into their life, they will have nothing to criticize.
For Jesus is the way, the truth, and the life that leads to love.
This kind of love is what they seek, it only comes from above.

William T. Smith

ONE BAD APPLE

There is an old saying that we all know is true.
One bad apple will ruin the whole barrel in a hurry.
This saying is also true in a church, or in your life.
One sin is all it takes to destroy the whole body.
When the head of an organization starts proclaiming;
What they say goes to all parts of the organization.
No matter if it is a church— government— or person.
What you do does not affect you, but everyone around you.
One sin in the church will cause a lot of unbelief.
The same goes for the government with one bad decision.
All this will cause unrest within the home, church, or country.
So, one bad apple, or one bad decision, or just one sin;
Will affect you and everyone else you have contact with.
We see this in our family, in our government, and in our church.
This is why nothing seems to be going well here on this earth.
No one believes Jesus is God in the flesh, so we all do sin.
Satan is the bad apple in the Christian life with Jesus our Savior.
We must remove Satan from our thoughts and life, in Jesus' name.

William T. Smith

GO THE EXTRA MILE

What did Jesus mean when he said "go the extra mile"?
When you go the extra mile, will you go with a smile?
So, what does this statement really mean in life today?
It means that you should do what is more than necessary.
When you hear of someone that you can help that is in need.
Go the extra mile by showing them that you care with your deed.
Even though that is not what we are taught in the world today.
We are taught: take what you want, no matter what others say;
Kick him hard now while he is vulnerable, keep him down.
This type of doctrine is not good, neither it is very sound.
Help your neighbor in their trouble, no matter what sex or race.
Not for your comfort or prestige, but: for their comfort and taste.
It should never make any difference if that person is a friend or a foe.
But: do it for the kingdom of God, in the Bible, it has been told.

William T. Smith

WHAT IS HOSPICE

In the world around us, many people are volunteering.
I volunteer for hospice; I believe my Lord put me there.
A hospice nurse put some myths and truths in the paper.
When you hear a myth, it may sound to be a bit bitter.

Is this a myth? Hospice is for the last days of a person's life.
In truth, the sooner you do the better, while there is still some hope;
To have a better life, where the pain is controlled and maybe recover.
This also takes a load off of the family, where there is a heavy burden.

Is this a myth? A hospice is a place where a patient must go to.
In truth, hospice goes wherever the patient calls their home.
Be that in their own home, nursing home, or even long-term care.
Wherever the patient calls home, that is where we will be.

Is this a myth? Choosing hospice means you're giving up on life.
In truth, you don't give up on life, but: it brings excitement and luck.
You will be living your days in comfort, with a lot less physical pain.
Is there something you wish to do; making a wish foundation will help?

Is this a myth? Hospice is only for cancer or those on their deathbed? In truth, it is for different types of diseases, including dementia patients; Alzheimer's, chronic obstructive pulmonary disease (COPD). And for many other diseases that may have no cure, we help in their comfort.

Hospice is an organization that wishes to help those patients in pain. The volunteers do their best to give comfort and companionship to them. We don't ask for anything in return, for it is our pleasure to help you. All we do ask is that you be patient with us in this task with your loved one.

William T. Smith

MEASURING UP

How do we measure up with all the things we say or do?
Do we take the responsibility for the actions that we do?
Do we blame someone or something for our actions and use?
Do we try and keep it under the rug, hoping no one has a clue?

When on the job, how are we measuring up with the work?
Is this job done responsibly, or do we just scrounge about it?
Hoping the boss or supervisor will not see us being just idle.
Are we really working for our pay, or do we just want a handout?

Do we plan on having a family, and raising our children with honor?
Will you want the best for them, while letting them have fun with you?
When you send them to school, are you corresponding with the teachers?
Are you helping them to learn, not only with school but with religion?

We start to measure up when we respect others and their property.
Respect their culture, their religion, their belongings, and upbringing.
How are we measuring up in this country or the world we live in?
Do we respect our country or world, does our country or world respect us?

Do you like living free with others, or do you plan on living behind bars?
We must learn to take responsibility for our actions, and respect others.
When we do, we know that only we are to blame, only you and I.
Measure up, be responsible, have respect, and live with love and peace.

William T. Smith

RECONCILIATION

What happens when you reconcile with something?
You come into an agreement to be the same.
When you reconcile your bank statement every month,
You want your checkbook to balance with your statement.
When you try and reconcile with your spouse in a marriage,
You become one with your spouse for that is what the Bible says.
You have a disagreement at work that needs to be reconciled,
With this, you agree to the policies of the company that you work for.
That is what we are doing when we accept Jesus as our Savior.
We must become one with Jesus, and work with Him in his labor.
We reconcile our life to live with him and die unto his death.
So that we die naturally, we are dying unto His life.
That is when our reconciliation with Jesus lets us be in Glory.
When Jesus says, "Well done the good and faithful servant".
When we accept Jesus as our Savior, we enter into His Grace.
When we die, we enter into Jesus' heaven and into His Glory.

William T. Smith

SUN-RAYS

My grandchildren are like sunrays to my heart and soul.
They may be small, but be assured, they are very bold.
They don't mind telling you their mind or what they think.
I realized in my heart that day, they were my missing link.
I was missing something after all my children grew up.
My life seemed empty, I had no joy and definitely no luck.
I realized I was missing the pity patter of little bitty feet.
And the messy face and hands when they played and ate.
It was helping them to learn to walk, as they were crawling.
Wiping their runny nose, and consoling them as they were bawling.
My grandchildren did put back this joy and luck into my life.
They will grow up and leave their nest, and all I can do is sigh.
Little children in my life are what keeps me going, this I miss most.
I know there will be children in glory, of this the Bible does boast.

William T. Smith

ME A PASTOR

A pastor once told me, that a pastor I should be.
So, I went off to college, a pastor, this I must see.
After being there studying the Bible for over a year,
A pastor I knew is not what the Lord wanted of me.
I was very sad when I realized this and cried a tear.
The Lord had a plan for me, the future was not clear.
It took me six long years before I finally realized.
Salvation is a gift from God, buying this I cannot.
Yes: this salvation is free to all that in Jesus, believe.
There is a job in the Kingdom of God for you and me.
After thirty years of searching, praying, and being torn,
I found it to be the writing of these thoughts or poems.
This is the one thing I never even considered at all.
Do not give up, if at first, it seems that you miss the call.
Jesus has a plan, keep working at what you are doing.
Before long, the job Jesus wants, you will be pursuing.

William T. Smith

Book
TWO

WHO AM I?

I was asked one day: "who or what do you think you are;
A great poetic author who thinks that your book will soar?"
I quickly said NO! "I am only listening to a small voice;
who is proclaiming Jesus is Lord with this thoughtful choice.
I am on a mission to declare for God, the name of Christ Jesus."
Just think of all that Jesus did, like dying on a cruel cross for us.
I want all my thoughts to give glory to Jesus, God's only son.
My prayer is this: Let Jesus come into your heart and soul as one.
I cannot find anyone that can do anything in their own merit.
I declare Jesus in my writing, this is the way I will always say it.
So, this is my answer to: Who or what I am, as you have asked!
I am a person who has given his heart, soul and life to Jesus Christ.

William T. Smith

MY SIX GRANDCHILDREN

My grandchildren are the apple of my eye, the glory of all this.
I started with two, then three, to five and now it has grown to six.
They are all different, they are all beautiful and very wonderful.
I love them all, even during the rough times, for they are adorable.
The two oldest are going on seven and doing very well in school.
The third is going on five, a very good big brother for sure.
The next two will be four, they like to play and going outdoors.
The sixth one will be two, and is already acting like a little lady.
At a family function, all six play together, which makes me glow.
One of the things I like is that they all want to be like their parents.
I am getting to know them, with their different types of personalities.
I thank God that none of the six right now wants to act like me.
I love them very much, and their heart to me has already been won.
I pray that here on Earth they are happy, and meet me in glory as one.

William T. Smith

HELL

I hear people saying, "Leave me alone, I like it this way;
I want to go to hell, all my friends are there," they say.
Do they really know what they are saying about this awful place?
Do they really think they will have friends there for their case?
Do you have any idea what hell is and what you will be doing?
Hell is a place of punishment, and that is what you are pursuing.
Hell is a place of torment, with a body that will not ever die.
It is not a pleasant place for you to visit, let alone a place to abide.
The friends you have here on Earth, will be your worst enemy there.
Hell is ruled by Lucifer or Satan with no friends for you to share.
You may ask; "Who is Satan?" Why is he so powerful and evil?
Lucifer is an archangel that fell from Heaven and hates all people.
He wanted to sit on the Mercy Seat of God, instead of taking care of it.
Lord Jesus, the Son of God on earth, is the only one that can sit on it.
Satan could not sit there, he has no love for God, or his creation.
So: being in hell will be worse than being in solitude in any prison.
Hell is hatred, loneliness, and no hope. With darkness worse than night.
Do you still wish to go to a place like that, where there is no hope of light?
Come to Jesus now while you have hope, and let Jesus be your guide.
For no matter what comes about, He will never leave you from his side.

William T. Smith

CHRISTIAN PRAY

I understand that there is a lot of Christmas in the world today.
Let us please come together, and reason with our Lord and pray.
Being our sins are as scarlet, we know they can be white as snow.
Though our sins are as crimson, Jesus said they shall be as wool.
If we are willing to be obedient and put all our trust in Lord Jesus.
The riches of this land, will belong to the United States of America.
The way things are now, we are being devoured by other nations.
Aliens coming across our borders as illegals, in many locations.
The jobs we need for our people are going across the seas of the world.
Where there are no jobs, there are no taxes, no taxes no government.
But: if we turn back to the Lord, Jesus will heal our great nation.
We need to forget about the lies of our elected politicians, we need truth.
Go back to the way it was when we let our Lord be the God of the United
States.
But now sin is lurking in every corner, especially in high government.
Remember where we came from, remember when we worshiped Jesus.
We need to start praying, so this nation of ours will not fall away within.
A Godly nation will be the leader that other nations look up to and copy.
We are failing in that responsibility to our Lord Jesus and our citizens.

William T. Smith

LEAD ME, LORD

There is a gospel song that I like very well; Lead me, Lord.
When I sing this song, I really do want my Lord's leading.
When Jesus leads me, it sometimes takes me to weird places.
That somewhere may be at home, in the country, or on foreign soil.
It may be to a member of a family, or to a passing stranger.
Sometimes it will be somewhere you may think is appalling.
Like a dance hall, a bar, or maybe a game of some sort.
If you are being led by Jesus, no matter what, you will succeed.
When Jesus leads you to these places that are very uncomfortable.
Be of good cheer, for someone is ready to receive God's word.
Which means they are ready to receive Jesus into their heart.
There is no way YOU can redeem a soul for Jesus your Lord.
If you are not willing to go and do, where Jesus says to go and do.
Jesus said: "Come unto me all that labor, and laden with trouble,
And I (Jesus) will cleanse them of all their righteousness".
Jesus: please let your spirit lead me where ever you wish me to go.
Your kingdom is more important than the world or even myself.

William T. Smith

LET GOD HAVE DOMINION

For God to have dominion in your life and be supreme.
You must let Jesus have authority in everything you do.
Dominion means: Lord God has absolute ownership.
Your finance, your body, and don't forget your lips.
God gave man dominion over the things of this earth.
We have authority over everything here starting at birth.
What does that really mean? We are to be stewards to God.
A good steward will manage the affairs of his master's affairs.
God is our master; How well are we taking care of his earth?
That is the question that each of us must answer in our lifetime.
Each individual has a job to do, that only that person can do.
Are we paying so much attention to ourselves, that we forget?
God wants us to take care of everything he puts us in charge of.
That includes this earth, as well as the human life here on earth.
The human life is the most important of all our responsibilities.
For the human is the only one with a soul that will be judged.
God has dominion and glorifies his Son, Jesus Christ while on Earth.
When we magnify His name, let it be in taking care of his earth.
Remember that all life matters, be it animal, or human life.
God created all life for a purpose, destroying life is wrong.

William T. Smith

WAS JESUS POOR?

When we read Matthew 8:20, Jesus had this to say;
The foxes have holes, and the birds of the air have nests.
But the Son of Man hath not where to lay his head.
So why did the Son of Man when sleeping have no place?
The people in that community had to know who Jesus is.
They loved him when he was healing, and casting out devils.
But at this time, they rejected Jesus for saying- Son of God, am I?
Because they knew Jesus was a carpenter and a son of the same.
He was not wealthy like the temple Scribes, and the Pharisees.
Jesus was what we call today, the middle-class citizen of Israel.
Jesus was poor because he came from the Father who has it all.
He did not have a place to lay his head, for the people's rejection.
No, Jesus was not poor, Jesus had his own place and business.
But he was poor at that time, because: there was no one to believe.
When you do not believe who Jesus is, or what he is all about.
Then you make Jesus a poor creator, who cannot help you.
Not because our Lord Jesus is a poor helpless person so to speak.
But Jesus will not force you to do anything against your own will.

William T. Smith

THE CHILDREN

Jesus said: "Let the little children come unto me".
God loves children, a death of one should never be.
Driving your vehicle in a way to kill a little child;
Is just as bad as killing that child with abortion.
The death of a child is bad, no matter the given age.
It is a sin or crime when you deliberately kill a child.
But: if you have killed a child, or done anything wrong.
Jesus will forgive you when you ask with an honest heart.
We here on earth did kill Jesus, God's one and only Son.
God did not destroy us for doing so but gave repentance.
If you believe with your heart and mind that Jesus is God;
and hung on the cross for your sin, as Savior of mankind.
Ask for forgiveness, and be in glory with peace and joy.
Then you will be able to walk with these children in glory.

William T. Smith

A GOD THAT LOVES ME

When things seem different from the way they look.
I look into the Bible, God's Word, and the Chosen Book.
Sometimes the answer is quick, other times not clear.
I go to my Heavenly Father, for he is always nearby.
I ask Jesus the Son to give me the wisdom that I need.
I do not cut or hit myself, nor do I beg or plead.
For you see I worship a God that really loves me.
The answer I receive will come for this very need.
There is always a situation like mine in the Bible.
At that time, life looks different and I am stifled.
But: that is why Jesus died on that awful cross that day.
To free me from the guilt and pain, for I was lost.
Jesus did not come to make things more difficult for me.
He came to pardon me, for Jesus paid the cost of my sin.
This way I can and do, have a home in glory with Jesus.
Jesus is with me here on earth, as long as I let Him be first.

William T. Smith

LORD, I THANK YOU

Lord; I thank you for all these writings you have given me!
You gave these to me as a blessing, to help others understand.
When someone reads the thoughts, I have written in a book.
My hope and prayer are that they may also write their thoughts.
When they see mine published; they will want to do the same.
Lord; I know there is someone out there ready to write their story.
I know this to be true; for several people have spoken of it.
These people that I meet; all tell me the same thing about writing.
So why are you not writing; get off your duff and get busy with this.
Now is the time to get it written; the Lord will help find a publisher.
My prayer is that you will write something, that is better than mine.
My wish is to inspire you, so you can inspire someone else to write.
The Lord needs you out there proclaiming His name to the world.
You cannot do this if you don't get started with your thoughts of Him.

William T. Smith

LORD IS GRACIOUS

To the one that loves Jesus, the Lord is gracious and kind.
Jesus is the only one that forgives and protects my behind.
What does he protect me from; all the things that cause harm?
You see Jesus has given me his light, an eternal alarm.
The Lord God knows when I don't listen and do wrong.
He will punish me, but with love; then I receive a song.
When I knowingly do something against His will and word.
His punishment is hard, for he will be silent and not moved.
My Lord does not like giving me the "silent treatment".
Jesus says, "I love you, that is why to the cross I was sent.
Jesus and the Father are the God that will punish and correct.
He is a loving God that forgives and forgets, He does not hate.
This is the day to do something great; ask Jesus into your heart.
He will lead you in a way that will please Him, do what He says."

William T. Smith

DELIVERED

Is there someone that can deliver me from this death?
Jesus the Christ, the Messiah: there is no one else!
Is there someone that can deliver me from all my sins?
Jesus the Christ, the Messiah: the battle is His to win!
Yes; it was Jesus who delivered me from Satan's death!
I know it had to be Him; I could not do this by myself.
Jesus the Christ, the Messiah delivered me from my sin!
Now: I have a home in heaven, a glorious place to live.
I did not have to change my lifestyle for this wonderful gift.
I came to Jesus just as I was, and He forgave me of my sin.
Jesus took my sin, my hate, my disobedience and replaced it;
He replaced it with love, joy, peace, and knowing I am His.
What are you waiting for, Jesus can and will do the same thing.
All you have to do is believe that Jesus is God, and ask in faith.

William T. Smith

Book
THREE

CHRISTIAN OR CHILD OF GOD

There are many people that say they are a Christian!
When you talk to them, you may wonder what they say.
To separate a Christian from a Child of God is not easy.
This can be done; it takes time and knowledge of the Word.
When you talk, first speak to them about the nation; Israel.
Will they say that the church replaced the Jewish people?
In another way, are they following the words of Jesus?
Or, do they wish to follow the ways of this earth, or world?
Find out if they are opposed to homosexuality and abortion!
Are they showing love to the person, by explaining their actions?
If the person is for homosexuality and abortion; then think twice!
They may not understand, or they may be a religious Christians.
A true Child of God hates the sin that is being done through them;
But they love the person enough to let them know it is wrong.
I would rather be wrong in this world of sin that shames me.
Then to be wrong in the sight of God, and land up in the Devil's hell.
When we get into God's heaven, it will be very glorious.
If we are in Satan's hell, it will be nothing but total torment.

William T. Smith

HEAVEN OR HEAVENS

God created two dimensions while living in the third.
While living in eternity; God created Heaven and Earth.
First: God created Heaven; this is the Angels' domain.
Then God created Earth, the home for mankind (humans).
After creating Earth, God created two more heavens.
The first heaven is what we call the sky or atmosphere.
The second heaven is what we call the universe.
This is the heaven mankind is trying to reach first.
We have reached the moon, and I believe a planet or two.
We will not be happy until we reach a new greater galaxy.
No man has seen the creator God, or any of his eternity.
But: Jesus said, "He was building us a home in glory".
When I die here on earth; I want to have that heavenly home.
The only way I can; must ask Jesus to be my Lord and Savior.

William T. Smith

MY BODY IS A TEMPLE

Our body is a temple unto one we choose to serve.
It became a temple unto Satan: for Adam and Eve's curse.
What we do from the time of birth, is in opposition to God.
Our body became a temple to Satan, the God of this world.
Jesus, Son of the living God, came to redeem us back to him.
To forgive us of all sin; can't ask for more than that from him.
He bled and died on the cross at cavalry, to pay the price for sin.
So now we can be in heaven with Jesus; trust him we can win.
I serve Jesus; because I asked and he made my temple clean.
I became a new person in Jesus; he washed away all my sins.
The righteousness of God is in my heart, my soul, and my spirit.
Satan has NO dominion over me; Jesus is the only God I serve.

William T. Smith

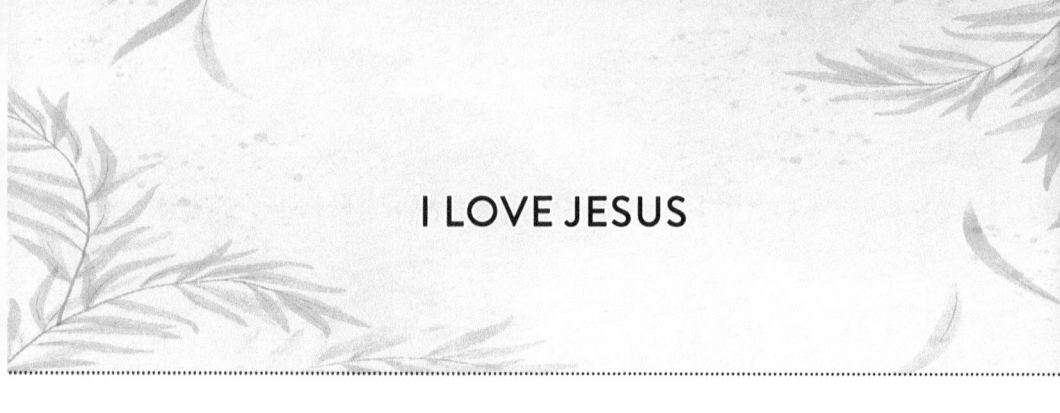

I LOVE JESUS

I love Jesus because he loved me first.
He loved me way before my earthly birth.
Jesus thought of me when he was on the cross.
So that my sinful soul would not be lost.
Jesus created both heaven and earth.
It was this way so he could break the curse.
Jesus knew what he had to do from the beginning.
The cross was the only way to bring the ending.
For a home he is building me in heavenly glory.
All I have to do is believe, let Jesus know I am sorry.
Jesus lives in my heart; I will live with Jesus all eternity.
For the sins I committed is forgiven, when I let Jesus in.

William T. Smith

OUR WORK

Our work here on Earth is only a test.
It starts at conception, and ends at death.
We grow and study in life and school.
We learn sports and even swim in a pool.
We work to feed and house, our family.
We correct our children to be law-abiding.
Our work on Earth will never be done;
If we do not teach them about the Holy One.
Jesus is the Christ, the Messiah, the Son of God.
Our work will never be finished, the son we forgot.
The work I am talking about is not what we receive;
It is not our possessions or money we accumulate.
The work is to know Jesus, and teach His word.
This work keeps the enemy at bay, Satan is a lure.
Jesus is our King; Lord over all the Earth.
Worshipping Jesus, should start at birth.

William T. Smith

DID CHRISTIAN REPLACE JEW

All the member of the early church was Jewish.
The twelve disciples and all of Jesus' followers.
These men went out of Jerusalem as missionaries.
But they could not be sons, until the death of Jesus.
The Gentiles were idol worshipers and unclean.
No one could have their sins forgiven until Jesus came.
Jesus started the church before his death at the cross.
How do I know this? I read about it in my Bible.
Jesus went against the Temple Leaders of old.
So, his followers came from the preaching of Jesus.
What did Jesus preach? Salvation is of the Jew!!!
So, undergoing salvation is of the Jew and not Gentile.
Then the church is a result of Jesus' salvation.
That means: the church and the Jew are the same.
We become adopted Jews when we accept Jesus as Lord.
Therefore, Christians are part of the family of the Israelites.
The Jews and the gentile Christians become brothers.

William T. Smith

LORD, DO YOU HEAR

I call upon the Lord, and it seems he does not hear.
I wait patiently, but it seems Father God is not nearby.
I pray to Jesus and Father God for the answer.
I look around to see if God is hearing my prayer.
I read his book, and it says: on him, I must call.
I keep living my life, and with it I am appalled.
It seems the more I pray, the more trouble I get.
How can I trust a God who ignores and forgets?
The Bible says, to give your troubles unto Him.
But how can I with this big awful load of sin?
If I believe in this name; the name of Jesus Christ?
Will the heartache I feel be gone, or cut to my size?
I do want to trust Christ Jesus with my heart and life.
But something is holding me back, with all this strife.
Please somebody tell me how I can let this sin go.
Because; I do wish to be in the arms of the Lord so.
So here it is Lord; I believe Jesus is your Holy Son.
Oh my: all my guilt is lifted; you race I run.
I have peace in my heart, I can forgive my enemies.
My prayer is: How can I help others, please let me.

William T. Smith

GOD'S ASSIGNMENT FOR ME

My job is to tell you about Christ Jesus our King.
My assignment is to write these thoughts about him.
My assignment though has changed several times.
The first was to raise my family in His light.
I did this with the best of my ability and knowledge.
I have been rewarded with a paying job throughout my life.
I did my job at work, and my family at home, the same way.
That is to do the job faithful and true as the Word says.
But: then I had to retire early from my workplace.
I did not know what I was going to do — In faith, I stayed.
I volunteered for Hospice, which I am still doing.
But the happiness of working for Jesus I was pursuing.
Then the Lord asked me to do something, write a book.
Me write — I needed faith in Jesus, that is what it took.
I put my thoughts on paper, not for me, all for His Glory.
What I received is a written book — to which I am not sorry.
For my assignment is to spread the Word of God with his love.
And to let people know — Jesus is with all of his creation.

William T. Smith

GOD'S JOB FOR ME

God has a job for each and every Christian to do.
The job, Jesus gave me was to tell my story for you.
The story I must tell is the story of Jesus' salvation.
How he came to Earth to reconcile the human race.
Jesus said in his Word; go and tell the people about him.
Tell them how he died on the cross and bore our sins.
Also, tell them about the strips he took for our healing.
All we need to do is believe he can, he will not forsake.
But the main thing he wants me to tell you is this.
Salvation unto Jesus is the only way you can be blessed.
It is simple, start by asking Jesus to forgive you today.
This must come from the heart, or else you will stay lost.
Believe that Jesus is the Son of the Living Breathing God.
That he came to Earth, for the sole purpose of redeeming sin.
Believe with your heart; Jesus died on that cross for your sin.
Then you will have the assurance of being in the Glory with HIM.

William T. Smith

DIVORCE

Yes: I did get a divorce; I was at the age of 55.
My wife met a man that was 20 years younger than I am.
I was very distraught and did plan for suicide.
But: when I got the divorce papers it made me mad.
Her lawyer wanted me to give it to her all; everything.
I would be in debt for the rest of my life, a sad song to sing.
Yes, I did get a lawyer so that I could fight back.
Here became a real problem; money we both lacked.
We realized that we had to put our differences aside.
We both, and our children must in this state live and reside.
We are divorced, we see each other, but we live apart.
There is peace with each other, while a new life we do start.

William T. Smith

IMPOSSIBLE DREAM

I had a dream, an impossible dream.
To see a book printed in my name.
I made a lot of mistakes on the way.
Thought I would never finish what I had to say.
There were many times I thought of quitting.
I threw it down in despair, holding back my crying.
Only to pick it up and start it all over again.
I know my reward would come in time, as planned.
As I sat and pondered on the hows and whats.
Lo and behold, I would straighten my thoughts.
I may never know or believe how all this came.
But as you see, I have my book here in my hand.

William T. Smith

BIRTHDAY PARTY

My grandson had his birthday party today.
His parents proclaimed: "It went well," they say.
There were pork chops with all the trimmings.
A decorated cake after everyone quit eating.
The water in the swimming pool was very cold.
That did not matter when the water balloons soared.
There was a bounce house, swing set and electric cars.
With a good size yard, the children could drive far.
The party lasted long, but it had come to an end.
The children did not want to leave, they were having fun.

William T. Smith

INSURANCE AFTER DEATH

Do you have your life insured? That is good.

Do you have your home and car insured against fire or other damages? Well enough.

Do you have insurance to ensure the education of your child or children? That's fine.

Do you have sickness and accident insurance? Good enough.

You may have various other kinds of insurance, but wait! Don't stop with this present life. Go beyond that: insure your life or death. You ask, how? Easy enough, and best of all, it's FREE!

Have the assurance of eternal life. The Word of God says, "All have sinned, and come short of the glory of God" (Roman 3:23). "For the wages of sin is death, but the gift of God is eternal life through Jesus Christ our Lord" (Romans 6:23).

Therefore, every one of us should be intensely interested in the question of how to find salvation.

Why will you sell your soul so cheaply?

Why are you neglecting eternity?

Friend, realize your hopeless and helpless condition. Repent. "Believe on the Lord Jesus Christ and thou shalt be saved" (Acts 16:31). "For God so loved the world, that he gave his only begotten Son, that whosoever believeth in Him should not perish, but have everlasting life" (John 3:16).

Study your Bible prayerfully (II Timothy 2:15), and "pray without ceasing (I Thessalonians 5:17).

And that, my friend, is the way to ensure your life after death and to have blessed assurance of everlasting life.

A GOSPEL WORKER.

If we say that we have no sin, we deceive ourselves, and the truth is not in us. If we confess our sins, he is faithful and just to forgive our sins, and to cleanse us from all unrighteousness. (I John 1:8-9). If you forgive other people and their trespasses, your heavenly Father will also forgive you: But if you forgive not their trespasses, neither will your Father forgive your trespasses. (Matthew 6:14-15).

Then spoke Jesus again unto them, saying, I am the Light of the world: he that follows me shall not walk in darkness, but shall have the light of life. (John 8:12). In him was life, and the life was the light of men. (John 1:5). The Lord is my light and my salvation; whom shall, I fear? The LORD is the strength of my life; of whom I shall be afraid. (Psalm 27:1). Jesus answered, "My Kingdom is not in this world: if my kingdom were of this world, then would my servants fight, that I should not be delivered to the Jews: but now is my kingdom not from here." Pilate, therefore, said unto him, "Art you a king then?" To this end was I born, and for this cause came I into the world, that I should bear witness unto the truth. Everyone that is of the truth hears my voice. (John 15:36-37).

For if God spared not the angels that sinned, but cast them down to hell, and delivered them into chains of darkness, to be reserved unto judgment; And spared not the old world, but saved Noah the eighth person, a preacher of righteousness, bringing in the flood upon the world of the ungodly. (II Peter 2:4-5). What do you think he will do the unbeliever, and those who reject him of today?

Book
FOUR

MY POEMS MY PRAYERS

These poems are my prayers to my Holy Heavenly Father.
In these poems are thoughts that I cannot cipher.
These poems are prayers of admiration to my Lord.
It's when I don't know what to do, in Jesus I soar.
These poems are prayers of faith in Jesus my Lord.
It's like a thread, but Jesus grabs it like a rope or cord.
These are also prayers of concern in many different ways.
I don't know what else to do, so in Jesus' name, I praise.
When I ask in the right way, I will get deliverance.
So, when I pray in Jesus' name, I do take a stance.
I stand-up for Jesus my Lord, He has given me what I got.
So, these prayers are for the glory of Jesus my Lord and God.

William T. Smith

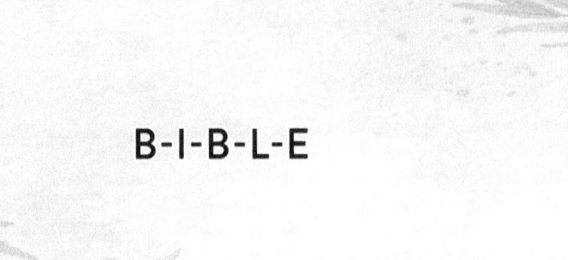

B-I-B-L-E

B-I-B-L-E: What does that spell? Bible, Bible, Bible.
This book was not written just for me; but for all people.
No matter what color, race, or even your background.
Believing in Jesus as Lord; is what makes this book sound.
The Bible tells us about this man, who is the Son of God- Jesus.
It tells how he took many strikes in his back to heal us.
How he suffered carrying that cross, that he was crucified on.
How he brought redemption of sin, that we all want and longed.
The Bible is the Word of God; not just a religious book.
When you read this book called the Holy Scriptures, or Holy Bible.
You will find it has many different subjects for all to read.
The funny thing about this book "the Bible" is when you read it.
You find there are many secrets, only if you decide to seek one.
You may read something a dozen times, and think you do not see it.
But keep on reading; the secret will surprise you when it does come.
But: you must ask for wisdom to understand the words of this book.
That is when you seek out the wisdom, that is when you will find it.
What happens when you get this wisdom, then you must apply it.
Things will be much clearer, just like God has declared.

William T. Smith

CONSECRATED SERVICE

There is a question I have perceived in I Chronicles Chapters 28 & 29.
This is a question for service, with the answer being totally mine.
Who is willing to consecrate his or her service unto our LORD?
Will you consecrate yourself just in the Lord's house or in your life?
When you got into a church or temple; remember it is God's building.
Do we do the things that will honor and glorify our Lord and Savior?
When you offer your service unto the Lord, do it with a willing heart.
Be it work; money or volunteering; it will count as a blessing on his part.
Where your heart is, starts your treasure, a crown of glory unto God.
Whatsoever God gives you in this life; rejoice for what you have got.
Our LORD GOD has made everything for our use; please use it for his service.
When you start thinking of others; you will be something special.
Always remember this; without Jesus, God's only Son, you will be in hell.
So, when you go to church; make it about Jesus, not just about religion.
For it should always be for Jesus Christ; any other reason is called sin.

William T. Smith

GOD TO ISRAEL- GOD TO ME

In the Old Testament, God was always with Israel.
When they worshiped God, he never did fail them.
But when Israel turned against Holy God Almighty.
Other nations put Israel under their authority or might.
In the New Testament, Jesus; as Christ came for all.
He did this with a virgin girl, Mary of Bethlehem.
Jesus had done this also by bleeding and dying on the cross.
Jesus arose on the third day; so, we can have life eternal.
The God of Israel, now is Jesus the Messiah, God to me.
As long as I believe in Jesus, honor and worship him.
I will have a home in glory, which is called Heaven.
I will be with my God, Jesus through all eternity.

William T. Smith

JESUS IS — SATAN IS

Jesus is perfect love — Satan is hate.
Jesus is the light — Satan is darkness.
Jesus is perfect peace `` Satan is turmoil.
Jesus is organized — Satan is chaos.
Jesus is warm — Satan is cold.
Jesus is a friend — Satan is an enemy.
Jesus is wisdom — Satan is a deceiver.
Jesus is grace — Satan is an ingrate.
Jesus is good — Satan is bad.
Jesus is a rock — Satan is quicksand.
Jesus is a lawgiver — Satan is a lawbreaker.
Jesus is always fresh — Satan is stale.
Jesus is successful — Satan is failure.
Jesus is tranquility — Satan is strife.
Jesus is total truth — Satan is false.
Jesus is heaven — Satan is hell.
Jesus is life — Satan is death.
You must decide what you want in life.
Jesus with all he has; Satan who has nothing.
What profit a man, if he gains the world and loses his soul;
When he looks up from hell and sees all he could have had.
Accept Jesus now as Lord and have life everlasting.
Or: keep Satan on your shoulder and be in torment.

William T. Smith

THE GAP THEORY

Have you heard about the movement called "The Gap Theory".
There is truth in it; look into your Bible, read it and see.
This is mentioned, use what the Bible says about this subject.
You will soon realize that God did ordain this gap in the word.
Satan was once called Lucifer, a great and loved angel.
When iniquity was found in him, he became Satan the evil one.
That is who showed up to tempt Eve to eat the forbidden fruit.
So, when did Lucifer turn evil? It was before Adam was formed.
Lucifer was to protect the Mercy Seat of God, as it is recorded.
But instead, he wished to sit on the Mercy Seat of God himself.
God threw Lucifer out of heaven, and as he went;
One-third of the angels went with him to the earth they were sent.
Creator God is a graceful, merciful, and just God.
Sin entered Earth and punishment had to be rendered for all.
Lucifer: now called Satan or Devil, in hell will be all eternity.
All who follow Satan will be with him in this hell, called the second death.
There has to be a gap between Genesis 1:1 and 1:2 for this to happen.
Otherwise, we would not be in a perfect world being perfect people.
We would not need a Savior, for there would be no sin to forgive.
But someone had to die for this sin, to those who ask.
These are the ones that refused to let Satan and his angels rule over them.
Jesus welcomes into his kingdom, all that accept the salvation from him.

William T. Smith

IS IT GODLY OR SINFUL

Jonah as the Word of God says; was told to go to Nineveh.
God knew what was going on there, from heaven above.
But; Jonah knowing how wicked that city really was;
And instead of preaching there, Jonah left in a rush.
Lord God rebuked Jonah, and still sent him to Nineveh.
As a result, Nineveh returned from its wicked ways.
The prodigal son wanted his inheritance early from his father.
So that he could go and live like the people of Nineveh.
He feasted with friends and squandered all his money.
He came to himself and realized he was hungry and lonely.
He went back to his father's house to be a servant unto him.
His father forgave him as he was walking up the road to him.
These two had different thoughts about the city of Nineveh.
One wanted God to destroy them; the other wanted to join them.
Sometimes as a child of God, we are asked to go where we don't.
The place where sinful people play, dance, drink, and show.
If we go there like the prodigal son to live with and like them.
Then everything is going to be evil, and nobody will be saved.
But: if you put aside your pride, prejudice, and differences.
And go where Jesus has asked, then a soul may be found worthy.
Always remember, it is not where you are called to go.
But: when you get there will you let Jesus be their door?
The door to salvation is Jesus, you must ask with an honest heart.
Jesus is the truth, the way, and the life; Jesus is the door to glory.
The sin is not where you go, but what you do when you are there.
Sin comes in when you do not proclaim Jesus as Lord and Savior.
For to know to be good, and do it not, to them is a sin.
If you don't do well, sin lies at the door, and Satan will rule over you.

William T. Smith

A FRUITFUL TREE

When I look at a tree that is full of fruit.
It makes me think of what David said about it.
A tree planted by the water will have fruit.
The leaves will not wither, nor break in the wind.
A child of God is the same as a fruit tree.
I am watered by the Word through the Holy Spirit.
I witness to others about the love of Christ Jesus.
Salvation is the fruit that I have, that is in season.
When the temptations and trials of life begin.
And everything I have is torn away because of sin.
I look to Jesus in this time of trouble and worry.
Jesus is my tree and strength; in him I will not break.

William T. Smith

CELEBRATE CHRISTMAS

The religious leaders of the church today say:
Jesus Christ, the child was born on this day.
But: there are other religions in some churches;
Declare this day, is the day Jesus was conceived.
The world has a totally different reason for this day.
That is: this day is for Santa Claus and his reindeer.
A pine tree dawned with gold and silver decorations.
With presents under the green leaves of the tree.
Christmas: what is this day really about, anyway.
The real reason should make the world sing and shout.
Not because Jesus came to the world as a little baby.
It is not the tree or the presents on this glorious holiday.
No: Christmas is celebrated for what Jesus did.
Jesus died on that tree, and rose to a new life, to begin with, you.
This should not be a celebration just for Jesus' birth.
But: we should celebrate the forgiveness of sin on earth.

William T. Smith

SPRING TIME

Winter is gone and now it is springtime.
The brownfields and grass are now green.
And with it comes allergies and hay fever.
While we suffer and wait for a stormy day.
When the storm comes and with it the rain.
We will get a little relief, as it may seem.
The pollen the wind will blow in the air.
We run inside and out the window we stare.
Springtime is the greatest season of the year.
Though I have trouble breathing, it is dear.
One day I hope the allergy I have may leave.
It may not be until death when Jesus I see.

William T. Smith

CHRISTMAS BELL

I go to church during this season we call Christmas.
There I find people worshiping the Christ child Jesus.
It seems to me that maybe they forgot the real reason.
It is not the baby, but: what the baby does for this season.
We should worship Jesus, because he did not stay a baby.
How could he have died from my sin, if he did not grow up?
We should celebrate his birth, but: worship for his death.
For dying: Jesus was able to take my sin completely away.
All of my sins, not just the sin I committed against him.
But: all the sins I do every day and not realize I need to repent.
Jesus rose from the grave, and took my torment in hell.
So that I can hear the ringing of that Christmas Bell.

William T. Smith

CHRISTMAS AT HOME

It was very quiet, quiet all throughout the house.
Everybody was getting ready for Christmas.
Mommy was in the kitchen making a cheese ball.
While Daddy was roasting the turkey, a butter ball.
Grandpa was helping Grandma bake fruit pies.
As the children were gobbling down the cookies.
The tree was quite big, standing in the living room.
We all knew, opening the presents was coming soon.
Uncles and Aunts will soon be arriving with cousins.
Where the quietness will disappear with having fun.
It's hard to wait, we want to eat the Christmas dinner.
The snow is starting to fall, it's looking like winter.
What a beautiful Christmas this turned out to be.
Waiting to open the presents under the Christmas tree.
This is the best Holiday; this is what Christmas really is.
Because now is the time we open all those wrapped gifts.

William T. Smith

Book
FIVE

I

I would like to do many-many things.
Where would I start, where would I begin.
To find out, I started to read many books.
I thought about exercising for my looks.
And all of this I tried doing on my own.
To pay for it, I would have to get a loan.
Do I have the look, am I getting smart?
The answer is NO! Books are the place to start.
After many years of trying all this myself.
I realized I couldn't with the book on my shelf.
So, I decided to go to church one Sunday morning.
This is what the pastor said in his sermon.
What do you think about the I's you try to do?
Is it what I want, or does God want this from you.
Try doing this, turn it over to Jesus, the Great I AM.
Give your I's over to the one that made mankind.
For Jesus us the "Great I AM" that it gets done.
Quit doing I, and let Jesus help you win this (son).

William T. Smith

CHRISTMAS

Christmas
A time to worship
God
The Creator
Lord
Of the Universe
Messiah
The Anointed One
Christ
The Chosen One
Jesus
Born of woman
Savior
Forgiver of sins
Deliver
Rose from the Grave
Lamb
Sitting on the Mercy Seat
Christmas
Glorifying God in the Flesh

William T. Smith

R I P

What do the letters RIP stand for: "Rest in Peace".
There is, only if Christ Jesus you have received.
For those who chose not to receive Christ Jesus.
Sorry, but you will never have this eternal peace.
If you do not have peace, what you will get is turmoil.
You cannot rest if you are tossed to and from.
You go into eternity, not having a peaceful spirit.
Once you are in eternity, your decision is final.
If you decided to follow after money, greed, and lust.
Then in eternity, you will be rewarded with eternal death.
If you decided to follow after Jesus, Messiah, Christ.
Then in eternity, you will be rewarded with eternal life.

William T. Smith

LIFE IS TOUGH

There are times when life can be very tough.
If you cannot get along with the one you love.
Do you think Jesus' life must have been tough?
Yes! Jesus made his life more interesting enough.
Although he did have a tough time with people;
To the point, he prayed to let his cup pass from him.
When we look at the trouble, or load we must bare.
You may probably think that nobody even cares.
But: take a look around at the difficulties of other people.
You may find out that your life is a whole lot easier.
For there are those that are hungry and homeless.
And staying warm is something that is hopeless.
If you cannot see any good in this life you lead.
Look to Jesus who can give you the strength you need.

William T. Smith

A BROKER

I looked in the telephone book for a broker.
There is insurance, financial, jewelry and others.
What is a broker, what does he do, you may ask?
They give information on what they think you need.
A broker is a salesperson, working on commission.
To find an honest broker, all I say is "Good luck."
When you or if you find a good broker in any business.
Then you will profit as well as the broker you found.
Never give up when all you find are self-interested people.
For they still may be able to find you a bargain.
Keep your chin up, and walk tall and with faith.
With or without, you still live, paycheck to paycheck.

William T. Smith

MAILMAN

Mailman, mailman where are you this day?
Mailman, mailman why are you being so late?
There is a letter that I really need to receive.
I look in the mailbox, but: no letter I see.
Mailman, mailman where are you this day?
Mailman, mailman why are you being so late?
The accident that I had, left me cashless, broke.
The check I'm receiving, in money I will soak.
Mailman, mailman where are you this day?
Mailman, mailman why are you being so late?
I sent a letter to my sweetheart for a date.
If I don't receive her letter, it may be too late.
Mailman, mailman where are you this day?
Mailman, mailman why are you being so late?
I have an important correspondence coming.
A dear John letter, it is me, she is dumping.

William T. Smith

POINTING YOUR FINGER

When you point your finger at someone.
Look at your hand and see what is going on.
Your thumb pointing up to release God's power.
Your finger pointing to the one that made you sour.
To let God, release his power against that person.
While you have three fingers pointing back at you.
That means you want God to punish you three times.
The power of God goes through your hand and back.
One finger out, and three back at the real corrupt.
You receive the damnation three times as badly.
But: your thumb pointing down is to release Satan.
Do you really want Satan to release his demons?
While you are telling Satan you want three times more.
Change your heart, and keep your fingers closed.
If you are having trouble doing this with your anger.
Give your heart and fingers to Jesus the great healer.

William T. Smith

WORLD'S FIRST LIE

God created Adam and put him in a garden.
Adam was lonely, so God created Eve for him.
Everything was peaceful, and very joyful there.
God would visit them in the cool of the day.
God said: "You can eat of every tree in the garden;
But: do not eat of the tree of knowledge in the mist;
For in the day, you eat of this tree you will surely die."
God left them to tend the garden animals and plants.
Lucifer heard all that God said to Adam and Eve.
Being Satan did not like God nor any of his creation.
Lucifer started to plan a way to deceive to mankind.
So, Satan said: "Eat of the tree and you will be like God;
You will have knowledge to know all things."
Lucifer was called Satan and wants all flesh to die.
Even though some were true: Satan told a BIG lie.
How do I know this: just look around at what's going on.
Everyone that is born thinks they know more than you.
Not only that but: how many cemeteries do you know.
Everyone born on this planet will die very soon.

William T. Smith

A CHILD

There is a true saying of a child in Proverbs 29:15.
You correct a child and he will be a blessing.
A child left for himself will only bring shame.
Correct your child when it is needed (Proverbs 29:17).
And when you grow old, you will have rest.
For he will be a delight unto your soul.
The Lord told Jeremiah not to call himself a child.
When you do my work, you become a man (Jeremiah 1:7).
Lord knows who we are before the womb (Jeremiah 1:5).
Which means we are a person even before our birth.
There is a time to be born and a time to die (Ecclesiastes 3:2).
No one has the right to decide that a life is worthless.
Jesus said: suffer not to bring the little children unto me.
Because such in the Kingdom of God (Mark 10:14).
The kingdom of God is the Kingdom of Light and Truth.
Jesus said that he is the Light, the Way, and the Truth.
Jesus said that whosoever received a child also received him.
Who receives Jesus receives the Father (Mark 9:37).
So please do not harm the children in this world today.
When you abort your child, you are preventing life from him.

William T. Smith

EASTER MORNING

This is Easter morning, as I climb out of my bed.
Get up, get up get ready to go to church I said.
We will go down and have a very healthy breakfast.
Then take a shower; put on our Sunday Best clothes.
When we get there, we will get a friendly greeting.
I will put a dollar in the offering, don't want to be greedy.
The pastor got up to give his Easter morning sermon.
As he preached and declared about the church decorations.
Jesus did not die just to be raised on the third day.
He rose from the grave so we can have peace in salvation.
All we have to do is repent, and proclaim Jesus is God.
Forgiveness of sin only comes through His Blood.
When we accept Jesus as Lord, we are free from sin.
Not free to sin again, but free from the punishment for sin.
We give our hearts unto Jesus, and we become a new person.
We still make mistakes but have a guilt-free conscience.
For now, we are not willing to sin, but we are asking Jesus to help us.
Jesus said in his Word that he would never leave us to be alone.

William T. Smith

IS IT OKAY?

People of this world say that it is okay.
To believe in Santa Clause and his flying sleigh.
With his eight reindeer flying out of sight.
Giving presents to all boys and girls in one night.
Which puts a strain on the parents to get that gift.
To buy the gift without having the finances.
Just to keep the Santa fable going on this earth.
All the merchants want you to visit their store first.
So, you go into debt for things you cannot afford.
Just to please a child that will soon be bored.
So, is it really okay, in a fable your child to believe?
Especially if the at the store you must leave?
Santa Clause is a fable, only a bedtime story.
Let your child understand, you cannot buy this toy.
When you cannot buy the gift of your child's desires.
They will not throw a fit and call you a no-good liar.

William T. Smith

ROBIN

Robin- robin- robin with your red breast so fair.
What are you doing in my grass down there?
I am looking for twigs and grass to build my nest.
I need a place that will keep me and my young safe.
Robin- robin- robin how many eggs are in your nest?
I have four to keep warm, to make a family at best.
I need to be on your grass to find worms for their food.
If I cannot find some worms, then insects will do.
Robin- robin- robin thanks for keeping company with me.
Summer is now gone and where you are going, I cannot see.
Yes, yes, yes, my family is grown and they are on their own.
Now I also must leave, for the cold of winter is coming on.

William T. Smith

Book
SIX

MY POEMS, MY THOUGHTS

My poems are indeed my thoughts.
It is my thoughts that you just bought.
You may adopt them as your own.
Remember the original, are these poems.
You may take my thoughts and adjust them in your life.
When you write the thought, let be of your strife.
You may have gone through something similar.
The experience in your life is the keeper.
My thoughts should bring out the good in you.
You should be writing about your blessing too.
These are to make someone else feel very happy.
Especially, when life says it is not very likely.

William T. Smith

NUGGETS OF GOLD

My brother wrote a book; "Nuggets of Gold".
It was never published: none of them was sold.
The beautiful poems that my brother Jim wrote.
Was about his life, the way only he could tell.
It is about things he knew, and hoped for in life.
But wealth and fame were never in his thoughts.
He could write because Jim had a love for words.
He did not want the credit, that belonged to his Lord.
He lived life in a way, he knew Jesus could see best.
He was holding his Bible close to his heart at death.
His children got together, and his book got published.
But: getting his writings together, well that was tough.
Don't feel sorry for my brother, he lived his life boldly.
For now: Jim is walking those heavenly streets of Gold.

William T. Smith

HATEFUL EYE

I walked into the kitchen one summer day.
A lady was sitting there and had nothing to say.
A very terrible feeling came over me from there.
I stop right there, it seemed she was staring.
I glanced over where I'd seen her, she was sitting.
I saw hate in her eye, and it was blazing.
This hatred was very strong, and visible.
It cut me through like a chainsaw cutting a tree.
My thoughts were: "Why all this hate toward me?"
I prayed: Lord gives me revelation so I can see."
At the supper table, we were talking and eating.
She said grace, everyone knew she was a Christian.
My Bible tells me; you know them by their deed.
Hatred in her eye, tells me Christ was never received.
I cannot judge this lady, for what it seems to me.
Jesus is the judge; she will know when she enters eternity.
My prayer is that she comes to know the Jesus I know.
One that is loving and kind, and does hold his own.

William T. Smith

WAITING

Here I sit, with my pen in my hand.
Waiting for the Lord to help me begin.
Should I go to town; or have a picture take?
Or: maybe there is something at the lake.
Will the answer be Yes? Will it be No?
Will I stay here, or will I be on the go?
The answer may come fast, or maybe slow.
One thing is for sure, only Jesus knows.
When the answer comes into bloom.
I will be back to writing pretty soon.

William T. Smith

SICKNESS

What is the main reason, a person may become sick?
It is mainly because of a war between soul and spirit.
Your soul as some people say, is your conscience.
Your conscience is where Jesus wants you to stand.
Your spirit is in control of all your wants and desires.
Following your desire determines who you really are.
When the soul and the spirit war with each other.
Your body reacts to this war, and your mind is bothered.
This is the reason most sickness comes into your life.
Because of all this torment, your body reacts with strife.
The rest of the sickness may be caused by the earth's nature.
The way you eat and act, at home, at play, or at work;
May you bring a peaceful soul, and a peaceful spirit.
When this happens, your body will help the sickness.
Put your trust in the Lord, and do what the Word says.
This may cause your body and life to be in total happiness.

William T. Smith

RAPE

I saw on the news, that a lady said she was raped.
I cannot understand why she brought it up 20 years late.
I am not saying that she was not raped by this person.
But: why is she bringing it up after his nomination?
Why did it suddenly come out at this time of his life?
Why did it not come out earlier, after it happened?
I know there could be several different reasons for it;
For this was not a family member, was counseling sought?
Today all that is said, could very well be called "hear say."
She may have a grudge or a different political persuasion.
If the man is guilty, he should definitely be punished.
If not; his accuser should suffer the consequences of lying.
Should we be putting a time limit on this type of crime?
On a lot of crimes done, there is a 7 years grace submission.
But: what I have seen in this type of crime or situation.
The man is always guilty, even when he is innocent.
We need to be careful of what we accuse a person of doing.
The life you destroy may not be his, but in reality, yours.

William T. Smith

MY FIRST PICK-UP

I got my first pick-up at the age of twenty.
It was a short bed, and I had fun plenty.
A six banger, and boy it had plenty of pert.
May only be a half-ton, but could haul dirt.
I could load it down, and drive where I want.
All I would do is shift it down into 2nd gear.
I had that truck for twelve wonderful years.
Had to fix it a few times, but I had no fear.
A pressure-plate with twenty-three cracks.
Got where I was going, but hard on my back.
I did sell it; thought I needed a bigger truck.
Haven't found another that gave me much luck.
The good news about that old half ton pick-up.
It was fixed up and restored to its original look.

William T. Smith

I WENT TO COLLEGE

Once upon a time, I went to ONC College.
That stands for Olivet Nazarene College.
The campus is located in Kankakee Illinois.
I was asked at first, "What was your grades."
Well, I have been out of school for ten years.
I cannot remember that, I said with a tear.
What kind of course do you plan to take?
A pastor of a church for goodness's sake!
So, I got registered and started my classes.
"With these grades, you will never pass;"
That is what all the teachers said to me.
A pastor is what my Pastor said I would be.
So, I studied and worked very hard, every day.
But after eighteen months, I could not stay.
For you see, a pastor of a church, I'll never be.
That is not the work my God wants for me.
At that time, I was not a child of the living God.
I never accepted Jesus as my Lord and Savior.
Makes me wonder, how many pastors do we have;
Is it like that, know who Jesus is, but have no relationship?

William T. Smith

MY GRANDSON

I was sitting on the porch watching cars go by.
With my grandson there sitting at my side.
I was writing a poem and being happy and glad.
As my grandson was watching something on iPad.
He cannot sit still for very long at any given time.
I had to go with him, so he would not cut a shine.
He is a redhead boy, and that definitely shows.
Always doing something, and always on the go.
He wanted music, he turned on the radio in my truck.
I tried to keep the volume down, with no luck.
He is not a bad boy, like all children, he's very energetic.
All he does is make my days very hectic.

William T. Smith

TREVOR

Trevor- Trevor- Trevor with that bright red hair.
Where have you been? Tell me if you dare.
I went to play at a place where I was very bad.
I got spanked, and now I am very upset and sad.
I am going on four, and I'm an ornery little lad.
I don't plan on being mean, just play and be glad.
I get spanked because my parents loved me so.
They are good parents, and I love them also.
I want to be free and not listen to what they say.
So, I get punished, and sometimes to bed, I lay.
So, I cry, I pout, and throw a temper tantrum.
But: when all is said, and the end of the day is done.
I throw my arms around them and I will say:
Thank you for your love, tomorrow I might behave.
I will never learn unless I do things that is wrong.
When I grow up, I know I will become a good son.

William T. Smith

MAMA

Mama, Mama, Mama with hair so long and black.
Not much education, but a heart filled with songs.
Who never worked at a job, but: she knows a lot.
I was taught more than any school about life and God.
Lord Jesus was with her in everything, every day.
She always asked Jesus for help, with what she said.
She was filled with joy, while singing at the stove.
She always worked hard, while singing like a dove.
Mama always liked and wanted to be with children.
She said, "You can always see God working in them."
When she died, she went into heaven or Glory land.
Where she is with Christ and His heavenly band.

William T. Smith

ARE YOU RELIGIOUS?

The church does a lot of things that are religious.
The real Church is only one; that is those in Jesus.
Jesus did not come so everyone could be religious.
Jesus came so everyone could celebrate a new life.
If we go to church and participate in religious sites.
To show people what they want to see on our site.
Then we are still living in darkness and in death.
We are still sinful people, as everyone says.
When we accept Jesus as our Savior, Lord and King.
We give unto our Savior, what belongs to only Him.
We see His beauty throughout the whole universe.
We are now alive and not under the sin's death curse.
Religion is great for morals that we should live by.
To get into heaven, we need to be the Church of Christ.
Christ Jesus said, "I am the way unto eternal life."
For eternal life, you must know the Son, Jesus Christ.

William T. Smith

PLAN OF SALVATION

What do you understand it takes for a person to go to Heaven?
Consider how the Bible answers this question: It's a matter of FAITH

F IS FOR FORGIVENESS
We cannot have eternal life and heaven
without God's forgiveness.
—Read Ephesians 1:7a.
A IS FOR AVAILABLE
Forgiveness is available. It is—
* Available for all.
—Read John 3:16.
* But not automatic.
—Read Matthew 7:21a.
I IS FOR IMPOSSIBLE
It is impossible for God to allow sin into heaven.
* Because of who He is: God is loving and just.
His judgement is against sin.
—Read James 2:13a.
* Because of who we are:
Every person is a sinner.
—Read Romans 3:23.
But how can a sinful person enter heaven, when God allows no sin?
T IS FOR TURN
Turn means to repent.
* Turn from something— sin and self.
—Read Luke 13:3b.
* Turn to someone; trust Christ only.

—Read Romans 10:9.

H IS FOR HEAVEN

Heaven is eternal life.

* Here

—Read John 10:10b.

* Hereafter

—Read John 14:3.

How can a person have God's forgiveness, heaven and eternal life, and Jesus as personal savior and Lord? By trusting in Christ and asking Him for forgiveness. Take the step faith described by another meaning of FAITH: Forsaking All I Trust Him.

Prayer:

Lord Jesus, I know I am a sinner and have displeasd You in many ways. I believe You died for my sin and only through faith in Your death and resurrection can I be forgiven.

I want to turn from my sin and ask You to come into my life as my Savior and Lord. From this day on, I will follow You by living a life that pleases You. Thank You, Lord Jesus for saving me. Amen.

After you have received Jesus Christ into your life, tell a Christian friend about this important decision you have made. Follow Christ in believer's baptism and church membership. Grow in your faith and enjoy new friends in Christ by becoming part of a church. There, you'll find others who will love and support you.

Book
SEVEN

PEOPLE OF U. S. A.

People of the U. S. A., come, let us walk in the Light.
Let's ask for forgiveness, and start doing what's right.
We have gone far away from our forefather's leading.
Turn back to Jesus, the Light: This poet is pleading.
Our land is filled with many strange religions.
People who say they know God, but turn a deaf ear.
Our land is filled with silver, gold, and other treasures.
We are giving it to other countries at their pleasure.
When are we going to wake up and take back our land?
From coast to coast, let her be strong and firmly stand.
This was once a great nation, one to be proud to live in.
What I see now are drugs, murder, chaos, and terrorism.
What happened to this country in the past 75 years?
We turned away from Jesus, and now reaping tears.
Jesus is in the business of forgiving; all we need is to ask.
Jesus will turn this nation around as He did in the past.

William T. Smith

ELECTION DAY

Election day: Did you vote and put in your say?
If things are not what you like, put your vote in today.
The person you voted for, as you know, may not win.
Just keep casting your vote, this is where you begin.
After the election is over, and you have your say.
Like the candidate or not, it is time to pray.
Keep all the politicians on yours and the church's playlist.
It will do better than doubling up your fist.
Remember this one thing about political office.
God put them there, they do have something to offer.
When their work is done, God will take them out.
What will your reaction be, will you shout or pout?
Nothing will change in this country, without your say.
Will you give it a try, it is your say, please go and vote.

William T. Smith

A BLESSED NATION

We have come a long way in this blessed nation.
As every person knows of the blessed sensation.
We started with 13 states on the eastern shore.
Now we have 48 states to the western shore, plus 2 more.
This is a land of plenty, and people are wanting more.
With this, some have figured they need to rip off the poor.
Other countries know that we are very well blessed.
Some want to come and live here; others just envy us.
No matter where you live; you can also be very blessed.
Turn to Jesus as your God, you also can be a blessing.
All you need to do is accept Jesus Christ as your God.
We will be blessed, as long as we do things God's way.
When the time comes when we think we are not blessed.
Look back at the ungodly things we have done, then pray.

William T. Smith

ARE YOU AMERICAN

There is one statement that I always hear.
I cringe when that statement comes to my ear.
The main statement is this: "I am an Afro-American."
The fact is: you were born in this nation, the U.S.A…
"I am a Russian-Japanese-Indian-Irish-American,"
And yet you were also born in this nation, the U.S.A…
I can go with every ethnic group in this country.
Why are you not wanting to accept, that you're American?
Are you being contrary because of your parents, or;
Do you think you would be better somewhere else?
It's your choice: choose America or your ancestors.
There are two ways to be a citizen of the U.S.A…
The first is to be born here, which is natural citizenship.
The second is earned or declared for citizenship.
If you wish to be an American, then act like a citizen.
If you do not like it here, fine go back to your ancestors.
A United States citizen has rules and laws to live by.
Obey our laws, not the laws where your folks were born.
No matter if you are Black-White-Red-Yellow or Brown.
American is an American; be proud, follow our Constitution.

William T. Smith

NATION OF THE FREE

There is a reason we are called: Land of the free.
Lately I have been asking: How long will this be?
The politicians are trying to take these rights away.
The people of this country want terrorism, they say.
Half of the first Amendment is almost gone it seems.
As the politicians are saying: we don't want religion.
The second amendment is going way out of our sight.
Taking our guns, so the unlawful us cannot fight.
The fourth Amendment will soon be of no effect.
The government can come in and seize without a warrant.
Article one section nine is being violated by Congress.
They take money from Social Security without permission.
So — Is Congress passing bills that is good for citizens?
Are they doing what is right for this nation to stay free?
Get your copy of the Constitution of the United States.
See for yourself, are they for you? Or for themselves.
Go to the polls and vote for a candidate of your choice.
Let's take back America through the elections of this nation.

William T. Smith

RETIRE FROM WORK

I could work from six a.m. to five p.m.
At the end of the day, be able to do it again.
I had a place to go and a job to do every day.
The company I worked for paid well, so I stayed.
But when you retire, your motivation is gone.
Wanting to do something, is a desire you long for.
You are old and sore and cannot work like before.
Social Security is not enough, and you need more.
Then you look around as you see others in need.
They have retired and now sleeping in the gutters.
If you wish not to end up like this, do something.
You may want to volunteer, how about the Hospice?
Volunteering will give you a reason to keep living.
Doing something is what will give you a blessing.
Bless you, in health and mind, for it will not be idle.
An old saying: Idle hands is the Devil's playground.

William T. Smith

BE A VOLUNTEER

The music is playing loudly, this song I hear.
Give your life to Jesus Christ, and be a volunteer.
What will I volunteer for? What can I do?
It does not matter when you take Jesus with you.
I may go to another country, and be a missionary.
If Jesus does not call me there, will I have a melody?
The volunteer work I do must be with the Lord.
For the Lamb of God (Jesus) in my heart is stored.
Be it on foreign soil, or in my country, my homeland.
I must declare Jesus is my salvation, Jesus must stand.
Be it in the community where I live, or at my church.
The hand of God must be there, He is my assurance.

William T. Smith

THE RELIGION FOR ME

When we quote the First Amendment of our Constitution.
Freedom of the press is what we usually think of first.
That does not mean they have the right to slander and lie.
It means to print the truth to the best of their ability.
The first part of this Amendment is what most people forget.
That is to be free to choose the religion that is best for me.
The government is saying that we should be free from religion.
We do not burn and kill those that do not agree with my faith.
This Amendment gives me the right to choose my religion;
Without prejudice, written manuscripts, or facing a jail sentence.
Just because the government does not agree or needs to blame;
the Biblical principles of religion, for the chaos of the nation.
The First Amendment gives me the right to assemble together;
Peaceably, just like the press printing the news for the nation.

William T. Smith

THE CORPORATION

The Creator of heaven and earth; formed a corporation.
It started when He gave mankind dominion over the earth.
The C.E.O. is God the Father; or Holy Heavenly Father.
The President is Jesus, the Son; Christ the Messiah.
The Vice-President is the Holy Spirit; which helps men.
I am therefore a manager; who carries out the commission.
First, my assignment is to carry the good news to others.
My work is to help others know the truth about Christ Jesus.
My assignment is doing the will of my Holy Heavenly Father.
The assignment I am doing is being a faith poet, and author.
With this, I also must be a faithful steward toward my Savior.
That is to take care of what I have; spiritually and financially.
Second, I must be a good teacher of God's Holy Word.
My agenda is to be a good dad, granddad, citizen, and writer.
When all of this is accomplished: I will get to meet my maker.
These are the words I hope to hear: "Welcome, my good manager."
You were faithful in the little jobs I gave you on Earth.
I will make you ruler over the cities I will give you in eternity.
Welcome into the Kingdom of Heaven: all Glory to God Jesus.

William T. Smith

THE C.E.C.

What is the C.E.C.? That is Christ's Electric Company-Corporation.
And the Lord formed man of the dust from the ground and breathed in life.
And man became a living soul, from that time on. Genesis 2:7
The breath that God puts into men is the electric current into the heart.
This electric current is necessary for the pumping of blood into our body.
Nothing would work inside our body with this electrical current flowing.
Solomon asked God for an understanding heart to judge his people.
God enlarged Solomon's heart with wisdom and understanding. I Kings
3:7-10.
When you listen to the heart of the world, your heart will be at peace.
When your faith is obedient to the Lord, your heart will be overjoyed.
When you put your mind to doing the things God said in His Word.
Then all things are possible with God at your side; what you do is: do it.
In all things, be faithful, obedient, and understanding; and never give up.
For in the Lord you will live, breathe, and move about the Earth at your will.
Always put God first in your heart, and your heart will always beat for Him.
For God is perfect in his ways, The Lord God is the only one that saves.
When you go with Jesus, God's only Son, you become an heir unto God.
Your life will be electrified by what you honestly do for Jesus your LORD.

William T. Smith

THE E.H.I. CO.

What is the E.H.I.? That is Eternal Health Insurance Company-Corporation.

And with his strikes, you are healed. Isaiah 53:5. He was talking about Jesus.

One thing about health is; the strength you have when you are healthy.

For the LORD JEHOVAH is everlasting strength. Isaiah 26:4.

This is the insurance that gives peace in all types of diseases and illnesses.

Blessed are they who mourn, for they shall be comforted. Matthew 5:4.

Jesus is your agent; the Son of God who forgives your sinful trespasses.

Thus, when you die here, you will be given a healthy body for eternity.

Thus, when you stand before God the Father, all he sees is Christ Jesus within you.

You shall live forever in perfect health with Jesus our Lord and Savior.

But you, who reverence Jesus, will be healed in his wings. Malachi 4:2.

On another the gifts of healing, through the same Spirit. I Corinthians 12:9.

There is no one to plead your cause; you have no healing medicines. Jeremiah 30:13.

Jesus will restore health unto you; because of others whom no man seeks.

Jesus gave them the power to cure diseases and heal the sick. Luke 9:2.

Wherefore I pray that you will take meat; for this is your health. Acts 27:34.

William T. Smith

THE E.L.I. CO.

What is the E.L.I. Co.? It's the Eternal Life Insurance Company.

We know that the Son of God has come, this is the true God of eternal Life.

We seek glory, honor, and immortality, we live forever with Jesus our Lord.

Our light affections work for us a more exceeding eternal weight of glory.

We hope for eternal life; God cannot lie; a promise before he made Earth.

According to the eternal purpose that he sought in Christ Jesus our Lord.

The Eternal God is your refuge under his eternal embrace of love.

Being He is perfect; He is the author of eternal salvation to all mankind.

Whosoever believes in Jesus, shall not perish, but he will have eternal life.

Only if you believe that you are commanded to eternal life in Christ Jesus our Lord.

The righteous of God, those who believe, will enter into everlasting life with Jesus.

Jesus is our mediator for redemption of our transgressions and sins against God.

For we believers receive the promise of an eternal inheritance.

I write all those things so that you will believe in the Lord, Christ Jesus.

In believing that you do know you have eternal life in Jesus our Lord and Savior.

So believe that Jesus is the Son of God, and have your name written in the book.

William T. Smith

King James Version:
Romans 2:7
II Corinthians 4:17
Titus 1:2 & 3:7
Ephesians 3:11
Deuteronomy 33:27
Hebrews 5:9
John 3:15
Acts 13:15
Matthew 25:46
Hebrews 9:15
I John 5:1

Book
EIGHT

PRAY FOR OUR PRESIDENT

Just as it was with the children of Jacob- Israel.
The U. S. A. citizens just want to have peace.
But: it seems as if the President stands for the nation.
The congress of this country will say "Impeach him."
But: if he talks to other countries and be a wimp.
Congress will applaud the President for being weak.
But: if he stands tall and holds to his convictions.
Congress will call him a bully and cry impeach.
We have been weak with a weak President, full of talk, and no action.
He does not stand up for the country and keeps us in debt.
Don't you think it is time for a concerned President?
Pray for our President, like him or not, we did elect him.
God says in His Word that He puts into power and takes out.
There is a reason Trump was taken out and Biden was put in.
Pray for the President we have that he will make the right choice.
For without prayer, this country will fall as Israel fell.

William T. Smith

ALL EARTH SERVES THE SAME GOD

I have found that no matter where I am on this earth.
There is one God that most people like to serve.
This god is not a statue or even something of nature.
But this god is a god everybody likes and fights for.
This god is bigger than you or I, we cannot handle it.
For this god will make you love it, or make you envy it.
The god I am talking about is the god called money.
The love of money is the root of all kinds of evil.
No matter where you go on earth, or what you will do.
The LOVE of this god; money will always have the rule.
But: there are some of us that do not wish to serve.
These are the ones who believe in the God of the universe.
We know we need money to buy, and love on this planet.
But: we put our trust in Jesus, and not in God(money).

William T. Smith

DO IT MYSELF

I tried doing things in my own power and way.
Sin always was there trying to get the last say.
If I let Jesus help me, knowing He is on the throne.
Love will always be there; I will never be left alone.
When you get discouraged, thinking that all is lost.
Look to Jesus, and the reason He died on the cross.
The blood that He shed there on Calvary hill.
Is the very grace you need, in order to be healed.
So, we all must quit trying to do things by ourselves.
Read what is in the Bible, don't leave it on the shelf.
Look into God's Holy Word; this is where life begins.
Only through Jesus, we can win and be washed clean.

William T. Smith

COUNTERPRODUCTIVE

Most people let others see what is on the outside.
They dress well and go places for appearance, it's a lie.
When a clerk is behind the counter; we only see the top.
When the clerk is away from the counter; we see all.
Most Christians are performing from behind the counter.
They don't want people to know that they were a sinner.
So, they walk in their daily life, hoping no one will see.
It never works that way; people already know how you are.
It is not our appearance that we should be worried about.
It is an inner person screaming, I want out, please let me out.
God already knows you are His, let them see Jesus, the "I am."
You were a sinner facing death; now being saved as a Christian.
We all have made mistakes in our life here on this earth.
We can only be perfect with Jesus, Born again, a new birth.
New spiritual birth is what Jesus said His followers have
Accept Jesus as your Lord and quit being counterproductive.

William T. Smith

FEAR CAUSES SUCCESS

I started these writings with the fear of failure.
The poems I wrote, I had to do over and over.
At this difficult time, I had a choice to make.
Quit writing, or do what God asked of me.
My family is the most truthful critics I have.
After their review, I wondered if I should quit.
Then a thought came to me; who will read this?
Is there anybody out there that would be blessed?
The Lord spoke and reminded me what He said.
Do my will in your life, your thoughts will last.
Let this fear you have contribute to your success.
Do your best and I the Lord Jesus will do the rest.
The point is, do not be afraid to do what I ask.
Have fear but do not quit, and always do your best.
No matter what is in this life that you may fear.
Give it to the Lord Jesus, who will always be nearby.

William T. Smith

THE MOWER

I got the lawnmower this morning.
Halfway done that mower quit moving.
I thought a spring had stretched or broke.
But instead of that, the transmission was out.
I said; this yard looks funny only half-mowed.
I was told that a friend was coming over today.
When he got here with his mower and finished.
He wanted nothing for his work, that is a friend.
The grass is mowed and it really looks swell.
I will get a mower, before it needs mowed again.
The way the lawn looked, when it was half-mowed.
Is the way our spiritual life is, when Jesus is not first.

William T. Smith

LETTERS

I get these letters; it seems all the time.
Republican, Democrat, it is all the same.
Some wants to give the President honor.
Others want to degrade him, vote him out.
While Congress is spending our taxes;
And the country is going downhill fast.
Social Security we worked hard for.
To help the ones who are retired or disabled.
Foreigners came over the border without work.
The foreigners will be getting the Social Security.
My sister was told, after her husband died.
So, in each letter is a place for a donation.
So, they can fill their pockets, and I do without.
The letter writers are good at what they do.
Read the petition and see what pertains to you.
In most of them, they want you to say yes.
If you don't, you are considered a bad citizen.
These letters are all one-sided, only for them.
The bottom line is; money is what they believe in.

William T. Smith

BUILD UPON A FOUNDATION

What kind of foundation have you built your life on?
Is it a foundation of good works that you have done?
Or: is it the foundation of lies, greed, and distrust?
No matter what foundation you have built so far.
It is full of cracks and holes; it has all kinds of scars.
When you repent of your sin; your attitude will change.
Then you will build on the solid rock of salvation.
You will be grateful for the things you already have.
With that, you will have found perfection in Jesus, with faith.
The magnitude of your life will reflect the Glory of Jesus.

William T. Smith

WHEN I

When I was in school, we sang about our country.
We all said our allegiance to the flag; "Old Glory."
In high school, I had to pass the constitution test.
Before I graduated, I had to know about reading and math.
English was the preferred language, with writing.
It took some time to learn, but it will stick with you.
I talked to some students, and this is what they know.
I have a calculator, for math, and an iPod with a spelling check.
So: I wrote something in longhand for them to read.
They thought it was a foreign language, and could not read.
I think now I understand, why they are using drugs.
If we do not teach them to read and write, what is left?
The politicians today, do not even know the constitution.
No wonder we are spaced out and nobody knows anything.
It seems that we are not proud of this nation or its flag.
It shows, with our lame unconstitutional laws being passed.

William T. Smith

LET THE PRESIDENT DO HIS JOB

I know that President Trump is not a perfect President.
There are things in his past that he probably likes to forget.
Looking back, one can see, this is true with all Presidents.
The Tabloids always want the worst and forget the best.
Why do the tabloids like to print lies, more than the truth?
When they are not telling the truth, our trust in them we lose.
President Trump is doing what he can to make this nation great.
He cannot do his job as long as the press is always in the way.
He is trying to protect this country, which I believe he loves.
The press is mad because: he was asking for help from above.
Our President should want this nation to be great and powerful.
So let the President do his job, for our country and your sake.

William T. Smith

TROUBLE IN THE USA

The citizens are being oppressed in this country.
It started slowly, but now it is becoming outlandish.
Back in the 50's, the Bible was taken out of schools.
To be replaced with, "The Big Bang Theory."
The Ten Commandments were removed from courtyards.
To have morals these days is very, very hard to find.
We have people crying that they do not want religion.
Drug abuse, abortions, and sex traffic are ever so strong.
A run on the borders of this country is very clear.
This nation is being split. They cannot stand for very long.
The question now is: How do we get out of this total mess?
We must repent; tear down our strongholds and pagan altars.
Turn back to God, like our money says: "In God We Trust."
Do this and we may have peace again within this nation.
A country without God, is a country bound for failure.
A country with God, will end up great and strong.

William T. Smith

HEAR YE, HEAR YE

Hear Ye, Hear Ye: A cry to Ole United States of America.
You have forgotten what the Constitution has to say.
Our dogs know where to go and who their masters are.
Our cats will crawl up and lay beside their masters.
You politicians get elected and then forget the voters.
Oh, the United States of America, remember our heritage.
When we were outgunned, and outnumbered by the English.
Our faith in God brought us to victory and the victory march.
Every battle, every victory, was won by our Lord Jesus, not us.
We used to own our plants, factories, oil production, and business.
Now foreigners have control of our jobs, our property, and homes.
Please USA, please turn back to Jesus, the Lord of the Host.
He will protect this country that we should love the most.

William T. Smith

Book
NINE

POET

Just think about it, I am a published poet.
Throughout my life, I never knew it.
I was inspired to write by the Holy Spirit.
Now the only thing that I want to do is write it.
Some are very short, but others are very long.
They all tell a story. Some could be a song.
It reveals the way I look and perceive things.
Most of the time, I don't know where to begin.
I thank God for His help; then I start to pray.
In hope that the Holy Spirit will let me say;
Some things I want to have written down.
All these words and sentences, I have found.
To say something, that will please the reader.
That will also, glorify my Holy Heavenly Father.

William T. Smith

INTEGRITY

In this life, what have you really gained?
If all you get, is wealth gotten with pain?
Can you take all that wealth with you?
When you die? What will happen to you?
There is a poem by a man named C. T. Studd.
With this saying, what I learned means a lot.
"Only one life, and it will soon be past;
Only what's done for Christ will last."
Look at all the things the world has done.
Wars have been fought, and countries have won.
Autos, planes, and ships have all been built.
That is now rusting in a junkyard in a heap.
Look at Christ Jesus: see all that He has done.
He went to the cross, for eternal life to be won.
In the grave his body lay, being in hell for three days.
All of this Jesus endured, so in peace, you may lay.
When your life is past and put in your grave.
What will people say about you on that burial day?
Will it be something good that you have done?
Will it be about all the wealth that you have won?
What is done for Jesus, our Christ, our Lord;
Will be the only thing: God the Father will adore.

William T. Smith

BORN FREE

Born free, just like the wind blows.
Born free, just like the grass grows.
Born free, so I can follow my heart.
Born free, so I can reach that star.
Live free, let the beauty in me surround.
Live free, so that my words will astound.
Live free, live in a land that promises freedom.
Live free, to do good things for someone.
Die free, in the love of my God, Lord Jesus.
Die free, the glory land of heaven I will see.
Die free, I know my loved ones I will meet.
Die free, for at the table of Jesus I will eat.

William T. Smith

WHAT HAVE YOU DONE?

There is a writing by a poet named C.T. Studd'
After reading this, you will either feel good or bad.
"Only one life, it will soon be past;
Only what's done for Christ will last."
In this life on earth, what have you really gained?
If all you get is wealth mixed with a lot of pain?
Can you take all this wealth with you after death?
After you die and get buried, what will people say?
Did you live your life just consuming wealth?
Or did you live your life, living it for Christ?
Will you be remembered for just your riches?
Will you be remembered for your service?
Everything you have done, was it for earthly glory?
Was anything done to increase the kingdom of God?
Earthly glory will pass away after you are gone.
Kingdom glory will last throughout all eternity.

William T. Smith

BLESS THIS MESS

There is a TV show called: "Bless this mess."
The mess in this country is being put to a test.
There is hatred all across this great land.
Churches are being burned, from coast to coast.
Thinking Christianity will never stand.
The government is pulling each other down.
Which makes this country a sad place to live.
Because: there is beginning to be no peace.
This started to be a land of freedom from tyranny.
To what seems now, to be a land for terrorism.
So, we cry out to our LORD: "Bless This Mess."
When Americans are not even trying their best.
For all the things we know are bad and wrong;
We now say is very good, and is it our song.
For this country is not being blessed with this;
The only way we handle this is with a clenched fist.
Jesus: alone can heal this country; this messy land.
But: we must pray and put our trust back in Him.
Repent from our sins, and from this very hateful life.
Because: Jesus went to Cavalry, was nailed to a cross.
To pay the penalty for the sin of the world that is in us.
So instead of fighting, and wanting to kill each other.
Pray for this land, and start loving your neighbor.

William T. Smith

A NATION THAT IS LOST

Sometimes I get discouraged and think that all is lost.
Then I remember, I was put here for a reason, a cause.
This life that I live, keeps me in turmoil, being tossed.
It was for me, and you that Jesus was put on the cross.
What I am seeing is a forward generation, with no taste.
Children believe there is no God, not have any faith.
A nation that has representatives, but has no council.
Neither is there any wisdom or understanding in them.
What is missing is the "rock of our salvation" Jesus our God.
The rock we trust in, is not the true Rock, but is Satan.
Vengeance and recompense belong to the Lord Jesus.
We wonder, where is this God of gods that we trusted in?
Oh: that we should let Jesus be our shelter, our refuge.
People of the USA, be happy and saved by the "God of Truth."
Let us rest in the everlasting arms of our God (Jesus).
Let the Shield and Sword of the Almighty go before us.

William T. Smith

BE POSITIVE

When you start to do something different and insane.
People will criticize and say: "You're wasting your time."
If you listen to these people, you will definitely quit.
But a brave person will keep ongoing to completion.
Yes; some of those people will say that you are lazy.
Some will even say; "Why are you too busy to help me?"
Others will let you know that you are wasting your talent.
Some will let you know how much money you spent.
Do not listen to all this criticism that you may hear.
Keep your nose to the grindstone and get some wisdom.
Wisdom by doing, by reading, by studying, and by learning.
You will never know what you can accomplish if you quit.
Never let these words be in your thought; I can't do this.
Be positive and say, I know I can do this, but I may need help.
Your reward will come when you see the project completed.
The reward will be the respect from those who were negative.

William T. Smith

MY HOUSE

I have a house built on a solid rock foundation.
When the rain and wind come, my house stands.
I have a spiritual house built on a rock foundation.
Jesus is that rock foundation, one that is very sound.
In time, my earthly house will be in need of repair.
The roof and siding will have to be repaired or replaced.
The pipes will get corroded and plugged, and the wiring old.
All new pipes and wiring will be bright, shiny, and bold.
But my spiritual house will stand throughout all eternity.
Because it was not built by human hands; Jesus built it.
In this spiritual house will be everything I desire and need.
As for repairs, upkeep is not a necessity that is required.
Jesus said: "I go to prepare you a place"; that is in glory.
"That where I am; you will also be there"; in this eternity.

William T. Smith

WILLIE BILL

I used to know a boy, whose name was Willie Bill.
He would always sit at his home, on the window seal.
A lot of folks would say; "Willie Bill is very very silly."
Others would say: "You know Willie Bill is just crazy."
No one could understand why all this boy did was stare.
Everyone was curious and looked, no one seemed to care.
Everybody wanted to know, but not a single one would ask.
People would stop and stare, but the shade would fall faster.
Folks would ask: "What is wrong with Willie Bill, anyway?"
No one was interested enough to find out or would stay.
They all would run; when they looked over at Willie Bill.
It seemed as though they were afraid that Willie Bill may kill.
One day someone decided to ask, and there everyone stood.
They found out that Willie Bill was a doll made of wood.
The people of today are still doing and saying what's not true.
Thinking that Jesus did not rise from that grave for you and me.
God is an entity with vengeance for destruction and hate.
In reality, God is loving and kind and wants all to be with him.

William T. Smith

WE OF EARTH

We of the earth will die of sword, famine and plagues.
We know what the Lord Jesus has done and what he says.
In the book of Revelation; Jesus has foretold all of this.
For we have followed Satan, the Antichrist, the Dragon.
You have taken the Bible out of schools, and government.
You have killed your children, by your law of abortion.
You have disobeyed your parents, and the law of the Lord.
You are doing what you say is right, in your evil eyes.
Even now: you of earth; please turn away from this evil.
In this the God the Creator may let you live in peace a little longer.
But: The Bible is true and all of this will come to pass.
As the Lord has decreed it in His Word, it will be so.
Right now, the Lord is watching all of this evil that is not good.
Because of this evil: we will be handed over to the Antichrist.
The only way to escape this punishment, is to accept Jesus as Lord.
Jesus says in His word that; He is the way, truth and life.

William T. Smith

CHRISTMAS SEASON

Christmas: is the most glorious season of the year.
Jesus:is definitely the only reason we are here.
God as Jesus: came to give a gift to earth's mankind.
Born in a manger, a dirty stable for an angelic sign.
Because a multitude of angels declared His birth.
He is the one, bringing peace and goodwill to earth.
Wise men and Kings came to worship Jesus, the Messiah.
They gave Jesus; gifts of gold, myrrh, and frankincense.
King Herod tried to kill this child, whom we call Lord and King.
Herod slew all babies under the age of two, just to kill Jesus.
So: Jesus is what the shepherds, wise men, and kings sought.
Santa Claus is what the earth believes in: deer and sleigh.
An imitation of the real deal; is Jesus being a laughingstock.
Everything Santa Claus and the world wishes in worship.
Jesus Christ has done with His life and death on the cross for all.
Salvation is a gift from God, life when Jesus was crucified.
Santa Claus flies through the night with reindeer and a sleigh.
Giving gifts in 24 time zones, in one day, what the parents say.
Now is the time to believe in and serve one God: Lord Jesus Christ.
Santa Claus and his sleigh; or Jesus, the cross and resurrection.

William T. Smith

ARE YOU AFRAID?

Are you afraid of what might happen in life?
Do you fear what is going on, that you may lie?
Is your life surrounded by bad, you wish to hide?
Do you want to give up and are you thinking of suicide?
Has any of this got you drinking or ready to take drugs?
If you do, your life will be empty; walking like a zombie.
All of this can be very frustrating and very fearsome.
This is when you need someone that you can trust.
Look for a redeemer, that is willing to forgive this.
Jesus is that redeemer; ask and He will forgive all.
You come to him in prayer, asking for His forgiveness.
If you are honest, He will forgive and give righteousness.
All your fears and doubts will definitely disappear.
Jesus will become your King, your Lord, your Savior.

William T. Smith

HIGHWAY TO HEAVEN

You won't find it on a map, but a highway to heaven does exist. "The Roman Road" is explained in the Bible, and it tells how to go to heaven.

We need God's power because we have a problem with sin. "For all have sinned and fall short of the glory of God" (Romans 3:23). "Sin" means missing the mark or missing God's intended destination for us. None of us can reach that destination on his or her own because everyone is a sinner.

When we work, we earn money. Sin earns wages as well-- wages of death. Because God loves all sinners, He has provided another route: "For the wages of sin is death, but the gift of God is eternal life in Christ Jesus our Lord" (Romans 6:23).

The highway to heaven is found in Romans 10:9: "If you confess with your mouth, "Jesus is Lord", and believe in your heart that God raised Him from the dead, you will be saved". We need to confess our sin and ask God for forgiveness. To confess Jesus as Lord involves agreeing with God about your sin and your need for salvation. You must repent of your sin, turning away from the direction in life in which you are going. To "believe in your heart" is to place your faith in Jesus, trusting that He died on a cross for your sins. "But God proves His own love for us in that while we were still sinners Christ died for us" (Romans 5:8).

If you would like to have salvation in Jesus Christ, sincerely pray a prayer like this one, being honest in your heart and believing that Jesus is God's only Son: "Dear God, I confess to You my sin and need for salvation. I turn away from my sin and place my faith in Jesus as my Savior and Lord. Amen".

Share your faith in Jesus with a Christian friend or pastor. Becoming a Christian is your first step on the lifelong road of spiritual growth and service God desires for you. Follow Christ in believer's baptism by immersion and join a local church.

My version of John 3:16-21

And Moses lifted up the serpent in the wilderness, even so must Jesus the Son of man be lifted up: That whosoever believes in Jesus should not perish, but have eternal life.

For God so loved mankind, that he gave his only begotten Son, that whosoever believes in Jesus should not perish, but have everlasting life. For God sent not his Son (Jesus) into the world to condemn mankind: but that mankind through him might be saved.

He that believes on Jesus is not condemned: but he that believes not is condemned already, because he did not believe in the name of the only begotten Son of God. And this is the condemnation, that light is come into the world, and mankind loved darkness rather than light, because their deeds were evil. For everyone that does evil hates the light, neither comes to the light, lest his deeds should be reproved, or corrected.

But he that does truth comes to the light, that his deeds may be made manifest, that they are wrought or fashioned in God.

In him (Jesus) was life; and the life was the light of men. John 1:4.

After reading this you may want to go back and read the Highway to Heaven again, with Jesus; the Light; being on your mind.

Book
TEN

LIVING IN ILLINOIS

In Central Illinois, where I was born and raised.
Fields grow green, and the cattle in the fields do graze.
Most towns were small villages, cities in comparison.
Where the folks around town know almost everyone.
What each family is, and what they are doing and have done.
There is a lot of wide-open space, living in the country.
We travel to the countryside, livestock, and nature we see.
All in all, we do not differ from the big city dwellers.
We work, play, and live to buy things from the sellers.
At the end of the day, we go home by bus, train, or driving.
We all need a savior. Mine is our Creator God (Lord Jesus).
What is the god you serve? Is it things, a job, or maybe family?
Ask Jesus into your life. For all of His creation is blessed.

William T. Smith

A NURSERY RHYME

When I was young, I heard this old nursery rhyme.
It became a favorite saying that once was mine.
It goes like this: You may throw sticks and stones;
That will most surely, or most likely, break my bones.
If they don't, they will surely bruise my skin or heels.
But no matter the words you use; they will never heal.
Words are from the tongue, that will curse a broken heart.
There are two pieces, as it seems, that will be torn apart.
But I have found a way to mend this pain from a broken heart.
When you apologize and forgive, is a good place to start.
Go to Jesus in prayer; the one who can forgive and mend.
Christ Jesus is the one that our Heavenly Father did send.
Jesus is our healer. He can and will take away the pain.
With Jesus; your broken heart will be made whole again.

William T. Smith

EPIDEMIC PLAGUE

There are those who wonder, and may even say.
Where is God? I don't see him in this epidemic plague.
In reality, God is as close, or as far away as you let him.
To those who have accepted Christ Jesus as their King.
He is living in your heart, your soul, and your mind.
You are the one that is praying to God for mankind.
The plague will soon be gone: What then will you say?
This epidemic took many lives, and that are in their graves.
A loving God would do something horrible like this?
How can I trust in this God, and still feel I am blessed?
What they do not realize is why the plague had to be.
It is because God is Holy and cannot stomach your sin.
We think God does not care when disaster comes our way.
It is "US" who does not care, by not doing what the Bible says.

William T. Smith

OUR NATION

In the midst of sticks and stones and all the rubble.
This country is most certainly in very deep trouble.
Yes: the politicians and our other elected officials.
They are the sticks and stones of this nation that talk.
We, the citizens of this country, have become the rubble.
That our officials leave behind them, like corn stubble.
Question: How can this nation continue to stand?
When we are tossed around like the waves of ocean sand?
Question: How can this nation again be great and strong?
When immigrants do not want this nation where they belong?
Question: With all of this; How can this nation be great?
Let us come together as a nation, for this nation's sake.
Let the politicians complain, while not doing their jobs.
And in doing so, we become a split nation, a broken cog.
Being split, we will never be great, nor ever be united.
We are being defeated by our own selfish, greedy acts.
Yes: this nation can become strong, and can be great.
Let us come together as one nation; for our country's sake.
Let us get back to the beginning when God was first.
Let Jesus be known far and wide to lift this sin curse.

William T. Smith

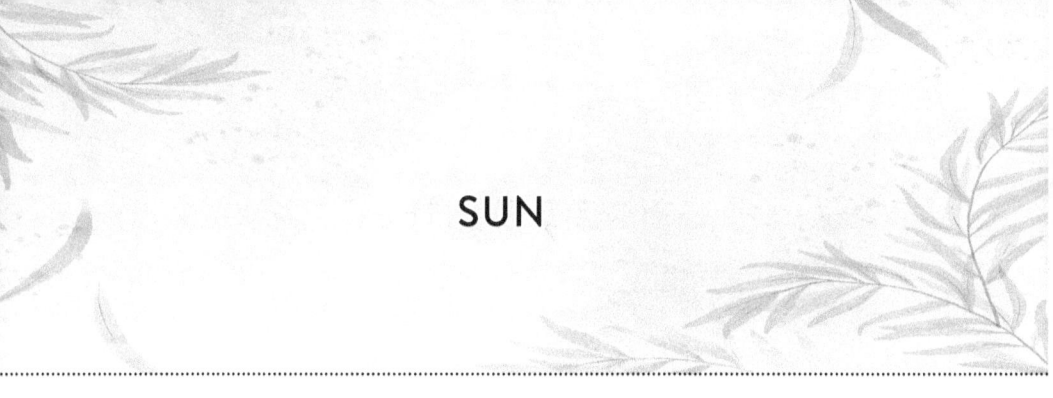

SUN

Hello Sun: way up there shining so bright.
Where have you been? Where do you go at night?
Why have you been hiding and out of sight?
I am glad that you are bringing back the light.
I have been in deep despair, my lips I do bite.
Wondering if I will ever see your great might.
For the warmth of the sun, I long to feel and like.
In the warmth of the sun and wind, I will fly my kite.
So Sun: I pray you will never ever leave me.
For when I am in the dark, I truly cannot see.
I suddenly realized that Jesus is like the sun.
I live in the darkness of the earth, with the redeeming Son.
Jesus came to repel the darkness, for He is the Light.
Sin is the darkness. Jesus came to forgive that sin.
Now it is Hello Son: in the heavenly realm of eternity.
I welcome you into my life as the "Son of God Almighty."

William T. Smith

WHAT DO I NEED?

Heavenly Father: I do not need a Mercedes Benz.
Or even a great big mansion on earth to live in.
I do not need cattle on a thousand hills to tend.
Or a really big farm, with many acres to keep tilling.
Lord: I do not need things of this earth to be happy.
All of this will keep me from worshiping you today.
Lord: as far as earthly things on this earth will go.
Just a place to lay my head with people I love and know.
What has the good Lord done for me and my family?
I wish to broadcast all over the land of this country.
For the Lord took the guilt of my sinful, selfish self.
And gave me a spirit of love for my soul to taste.
The things of this world I do not wish to cherish.
I ask Jesus to forgive me; I left it all on the cross.
So what do I need? All I need is Jesus in my heart.
He gives me everything that I need, and will never, ever part.

William T. Smith

CALLING SOMEONE A NAME

When you call someone an evil name.
Do you really know what it is you are saying?
You are telling that person, that they are useless.
Upon this land, they are nothing but worthless.
No matter what your color or nationality is.
No matter your IQ or your work, you are blessed.
Every person has potential and is a blessing also.
You look at all the things this person is doing.
You will see there is no person in God's universe;
That is useless, worthless, or cannot be taught.
Everyone has a talent or a very special purpose.
You are judging someone when you call them a name.
Are you so bad that you want to be like them?
Is that why you get mad and throw slurs their way?
We are all created equally by God on this earth.
Everyone that is born was born with a special worth.
When you set yourself up as their judge and jury.
It will come back to you in a way you will be sorry.
This is not just for humans, but it also applies to all God's creatures.
We can teach all mankind, animals, birds, and fish.
We can train them to do many things or just tricks.
The one thing that we cannot control or train is this:
The human tongue: you cannot control or tame this organ.
Like an uncontrollable fire, it makes you and others sick.

William T. Smith

THE VIRUS

The people who survive this COVID-19 virus.
Most definitely will find favor on all the earth.
The Lord God loves you with an everlasting love.
The Lord draws you with unfailing kindness.
Let your praises be heard, let your prayer soar.
God save your children, all that knows Jesus is Lord.
Lord: I ask you to turn this sorrow into gladness.
Thanks to the ones that have worked for a cure.
You will be rewarded. God will wipe away the tears.
Your faith in the Lord will be restored, come to Him.
Jesus: you are my Lord, you are my living God.
How long must we wait for your grace to be sought?
I know the Lord must uproot, destroy, and bring disaster.
The sin of this nation must not continue any longer.
Turn back to Jesus. Let Jesus be your Lord and Savior.
Repent of your sin and accept Jesus and His salvation.

William T. Smith

BEING WASTEFUL

This country is very wasteful; that I should say.
We have a habit of throwing our dinner away.
When we can use it for our lunch the next day.
Save your money, and eat leftovers, the saving will pay.
We throw countless of dollars right down the drain.
We do not have financial accountability, it's a shame.
We always have money for this thing or for that.
We never look around and see people doing without.
Just think how much better we of this country could be.
By eating leftovers, and giving money to the needy.
Our people have been trained to be a wasteful group.
Everything for ourselves, having no consideration for others.

William T. Smith

DREAMS IN THE NIGHT

Hello darkness: who has seemed to always be a friend.
I have waited all day, so I could talk to you again.
There are visions that stay in my head, softly creeping.
Leaving its seed in my mind last night while I was sleeping.
Been thinking about this vision that was planted in my brain.
Now that I'm awake will not leave, stayed here to remain.
In this darkness, there is nothing, nothing, but silence.
So now I can ponder the vision that I had last night.
In this dream, I am very much and have always been alone.
Walking these streets that are made of brick and stone.
I am standing on a corner, beneath a bright city light.
Pulling the collar into my jacket for this cold night.
I am looking at all the warm houses and cars that I have not.
Thinking: if only I had a job, these I could have bought.
As I am looking and hearing the families having fun inside.
I start thinking about my life. Is this all there is to be alive?
Jesus answered that question when He said, I give eternal life.
Except for a man be born of the spirit, he cannot be a part of me.

William T. Smith

AUTUMN

Autumn has surely made its way back here again.
The air is getting colder with the blowing wind.
The farmers are trying hard to harvest their crops.
They are going day and night, not wanting to stop.
The fields that were bright green, are now a dull brown.
The tractors, wagons, and combines are coming around.
Soon the fields will all be harvested and again bare.
The harvest is all done, clean-up begins for next year.
My prayer is that the farmers had a bountiful harvest.
You will be able to look in these fields watching deer.
The hunters at this time will be getting ready to hunt.
My prayer is that the hunter has a good harvest also.
Thanksgiving is around the corner with a big feast.
Thanking God for it all, as the snow brings a freeze.

William T. Smith

CHRISTMAS IS COMING

Christmas is coming, and all nations may worship the baby.
It is good that we remember Jesus and what the angels said.
But let's not forget why we are celebrating the season.
For Jesus came to earth, for the purpose of dying for our sins.
If Jesus died a normal death, He would only be just a man.
Therefore; no one would know who Jesus was, or why He came.
If Jesus did not die that horrible death or rose from the grave.
Then all of my sins and wrongdoings, I would have to pay.
But Jesus did go to that cross, and He paid my penalty for me.
He took upon himself all my sins so I can live with Him in eternity.
Yes: Jesus rose on the third day, from hell 's torment and the grave.
I did accept Him as my King and Savior; with Him, I will stay.

William T. Smith

Book
ELEVEN

OUR COUNTRY

Here is a statement from our 35th President of the USA.
President Kennedy: I believe strongly in what he said.
Here it is, "Ask not what your country can do for you
But what can you do for your country?". A true statement.
Is this what we are asking ourselves from this president?
How can we help the one God put in power? One God sent?
What we are asking now is; what can I get from this country?
Even illegals who want a handout, won't do things for themselves.
Is the freedom to be an American, a thing of the past?
If we keep taking from the country, how long will it last?
Wake up, people of this country – – we are blessed.
The way we are going; this country will soon be cursed.
Let's start working for a country, let's keep our freedom.
Instead of lawsuits to bring down; let's uplift the President.

William T. Smith

LADIES I MEET

Every now and then; I will meet a nice lady.
When I do, I try to let her know I'm not a mate.
But for some reason or another, should I not relate?
She seems to get mad when I say, a friend, not a date.
I was married for 26 years to a wonderful girl.
Then my wife divorced me, and I did shed some tears.
It's not that I don't want to date every now and then.
But I remember how my life was like a married man.
When I meet a lovely lady now; I just want to hold hands.
But it seems they think I should give them a wedding band.
My biggest problem is, I loved my ex-wife, after all of this.
So marriage is not what I am really looking for in my life.
One day, I will meet a lady that will sweep me off my feet.
Until then, I am happy being unmarried, with this freedom.

William T. Smith

BEING DIVORCED

When I meet a lady, I just want to make friends.
What they think is sex is the only way to get a man.
Others just want someone to be their live-in.
Now and then, one will try to get a wedding band.
I was married, and we had three wonderful children.
I got a divorce and my life got hard to focus on.
I do not wish to have that ring on my nose again.
I want to live right, maybe have a date now and then.
As a friend, you do not have to marry or have any sex.
Or try to explain the reasons for being a few minutes late.
I like my life being single, where I'm not pleasing a mate.
Not worrying about birthdays or buying the right cake.
It's really not that I don't want a mate in my life.
The reason is that I just do not want all the strife.
I have enough headaches the way it is these days for sure.
I do not want to add to the headache by listening to her.

William T. Smith

SANCTUARY CITIES

I have heard a lot about sanctuary cities. What are they?
The dictionary has two definitions for these sanctuaries.
The first one: A place or refuge for protection in a city.
The second: The immunity from the law, attached to sanctuary.
The Bible, in number 35, says it in a little different format.
It is a place a person can go for protection until the trial.
If the person is found guilty of the crime, he is punished.
If he is innocent, he can stay there and be protected by the law.
The way the cities and states have it surmised nowadays is;
We are going to protect him from punishment, no matter what.
Even if that person does crimes against the state or country.
A sanctuary city should not protect criminals, be a safety net.
When the state refuses to punish the guilty by harboring them.
Then that city or state is guilty of crimes against America.
Just because the person is an alien, they are not above the law.
The law is to protect the innocent, and prosecute the guilty.

William T. Smith

PRESIDENT NEEDS OUR PRAYERS

Our President has to make a lot of tough decisions.
Even though the Senate wants to impeach him.
I believe he is doing what is best for America.
While making America great, he is keeping her safe.
The president has a very hard and stressful job.
Sometimes he has to be like a car shark; holding the ace.
When it is safe, the people will know what is going on.
The president has to withhold information for a while.
So, we need to pray for our president and all matters.
If we do this, you may find that his job can be bent.
While he is in power, his job is to protect the citizens.
In doing so, he has to make difficult choices for us.
He has a hard job to do without all the added stress.
Please pray for our country and President. God will bless.

William T. Smith

I KNOW

I know that the world can take my life at any time.
Be it through murder or sickness, I'm going the same.
I know that the world can take all the money I made.
Con-artist and government regulations, in their pocket, stay.
I know that the world can take my health or life all away.
Believe me, on a stormy night, wondering what just happened.
I know that the world can take every bit of my belongings.
I know that the world can take my integrity and credibility.
To the point that I could not get a loan and lived on the streets.
I know that the world cannot take my salvation through Jesus.
The world can take what I have and leave me homeless.
My salvation does not come from the world, but from Jesus.
My Heavenly Father sent his Son (Jesus) to deem the world.
I am no different from you. We are all conceived in the womb.
Jesus gave us life and knows what we say, think, and do.
No matter where we go or what we say, Jesus keeps a record.
The difference between us is; I asked Jesus to be my Lord.
Jesus forgave me for the sin I did. Now, I am in His protection.
If you are making your work or your church, your Lord.
Look at what is inside of all your thoughts, and see if it is bad or good.
If your thoughts want you to do evil, you will not have peace.
Look to Jesus for your glory, he will become your savior.
Saved from the death of this world, which Satan brings with him.
To eternal life through Jesus, from our Heavenly Father in glory.

William T. Smith

PRESIDENT TRUMP IN 2020

President Trump has been criticized a lot during his term.
By the legislators that have done worse, we have learned.
But when we look back at the different presidents.
The one we criticized the most is the one God has sent.
President Kennedy wanted our strength to be known.
He was assassinated for all the goodwill he showed.
He is now deemed as being a great president in history.
The country back then did not know the whole story.
President Lincoln wanted peace and unity in our country.
War broke out and he was assassinated because of that.
His photo is in our pennies and five-dollar bills.
He is recognized for what he stood for by not quitting.
President Trump, I do hope you will win a second term.
This country will be praised and glorified very soon.
Because he has grit in his bones, and Jesus in his hand.
The Congress wants to impeach him. I don't think it will stand.
If that does not work, his character will be assassinated.

William T. Smith

PASSWORDS

I read this article by Nancy Carison Dodd on the paper.
Password to heaven! Forget your password and have a prayer.
even though this article was more on forgetful senior moments.
There is a lot of truth about a password to have a chicken sitter.
The fact is, there are actually three passwords to heaven.
You have to say these passwords in order, but here on earth.
First of all; the password has to be acknowledged in thinking.
Second; the password has to be believed in your heart.
I believe in my heart, Jesus is God; acknowledged in my mind.
I believe that Jesus died on the cross for my sins.
I believe that father God, son Jesus, and Holy Spirit are one.
I know I do not understand all of this, but with Jesus, it is done.
These are the three passwords you need to know here on earth.
You will get into heaven because you believed in the new birth.
The old birth is earthly, from your mother and her mate.
The second birth is spiritual, the Holy Spirit you must take.
The three passwords are very simple and easy to remember.
I believe in Jesus, his birth, death, and His resurrection.
I believe that the Heavenly Father, Jesus, and Holy Spirit is God.
I believe in one God, transformed into three personalities.
These are the passwords you must have for God's gift to mankind.
The gift of God is eternal life, through the Son (Jesus Christ).

William T. Smith

THE IMPEACHMENT

We are going through the impeachment of President Trump.
This impeachment has the country perplexed and stumped.
President Trump is elected; Democratic Party is mad, they lost.
Now, for everything they're doing, the citizens are paying the cost.
They have been at this for three long years and found no cause.
It seems they keep bringing in false witnesses that are tossed.
I have seen that no matter what the president does for this country.
The Congress will vote it down, the citizens pay the penalty.
When the president tries to make good on his promise to us.
The branches of the government starts lying and put him to a test.
America can be great again, but we must all work together.
As long as we keep fighting within, this nation will be split.
Our country, the USA, and the president needs our faithful prayers.
Not governmental control, but sacrifice and lots of tears.

William T. Smith

PASSPORTS

You have and need a passport to get into any country.
You have and need a password to get into your email.
You have and need a password for all accounts.
How far would you get if you left your passport at home?
Would you get into the country without your passport?
With our passports and passwords, we cannot do or go.
You also need a password or passport to get into heaven.
What is this passport or password that we need to enter?
There are a lot of words you can think of to use for this.
None of them will help you get into this heavenly blessing.
There is one word you need that has any worth.
You need to know this word now: I accept Jesus as my Savior.
You will have to let Him live and reign in your heart and soul.
You must give Him your devotion to your highs and your lows.
Here on earth, your password is peace, love, joy, and hope.
This will give you the passport you need for the Pearly Gates.

William T. Smith

MY DIVORCE

I got married to a beautiful girl, that is my wife.
For 26 years, I thought we had a wonderful life.
We raised 3 sons together; they are terrific boys.
Growing up, we gave them plenty of love and toys.
There came a day that my wife announced to me.
I don't love you and never did. I wish to be free.
It took about 2 years for the divorce to be finalized.
We walked away from each other without a tear.
When she told me, she did not love me anymore.
I became very lonely and hurt, my heart sore.
The Lord God did not take away the love I had for her.
But He took away the feelings I had or my desire.
I became a Christian. God didn't take away worldly love.
What He did was take away my desire for the world.
When I received salvation, Jesus gave me a new birth.
What He has done was take away my desires on this earth.
I still love this earth, as I still love my ex-wife.
I do not desire this earth, nor do I desire my ex-wife.
I do not have a home on earth, where I can go to be with a wife.
I do have a home in glory, where I hope to see my ex-wife.

William T. Smith

OFF TO SCHOOL

No matter if it rains or even if it snows.
Off to school this day, you must still go.
You need to study hard, or never get a job.
This you do to be a lawyer, doctor, or a cop.
The money you make is not your success.
It is living right and doing your very best.
Get a good job, make money, and live well.
Do it legally, or end up in prison or a jail
The school will not give you integrity in life.
That comes by knowing Jesus and strife.
To know Jesus, you must have a relationship.
You receive integrity you need to forgive.
When you forgive others despite their mistakes to you.
Then Jesus will forgive your mistakes to Him.
A mistake becomes a sin when you do it willingly.
You must repent from your mistakes or your sin.

William T. Smith

Book
TWELVE

A PROMISE

A promise is a thoughtful desire to do something.
When you fulfill that promise, peace, and joy it brings.
When I say — I do promise to do this or that thing.
Life may get in the way, and the promise is off track.
Can a person really keep the promise they make?
Yes! But the promise that better be heartfelt.
If you promise something, that you plan not to keep.
It is not a promise, but a lie your mouth does seep.
Jesus made several promises, and he keeps them, that is true.
One of those is the salvation of your sins, for me and you.
He promised a life filled with love, joy, and peace.
To obtain this, you must believe in the promise.
The Bible says: Jesus is the way, the truth, and the door.
When you walk in his promise, you will want more.
Jesus promised that following him would not be easy.
Satan will tempt you at every turn. Tell him to get out; flee.
Jesus will help you with all you do. Just stay busy and pray.
Jesus promised he would never leave you nor forsake you.
Jesus also promised that you would be in heaven or glory.
At the end of your life, and you see Jesus' face, no sorrow.

William T. Smith

ISRAEL

To Jacob, the son of Isaac: twelve sons were born.
God used these twelve for a nation, but they were warned.
If you follow after me, I will make you a great nation.
If you turn against me, I will give you trouble in your sin.
This nation started out as slaves; doing what they were told.
Along came a man to redeem them from that slavery; Moses.
Moses spent forty years in the wilderness preparing them.
When Moses died, a man called Joshua kept them from sin.
After that, there came a lot of judges, the last one being Samuel.
These judges kept Israel out of the slavery yoke of nations.
Then the children of Jacob; wanted a king to rule over them.
A king they got, the nation became great, for a season or time.
But God had his nation taken away from the children of Israel.
They were scattered throughout the earth; where no one can tell.
One day, God brought this nation back together again in 1948.
Jesus is fighting their battles, and they will win all that is fought.

COVERING UP A LIE

Sarah laughed when she was told she would bear a child.
Thinking, how can I have a child in my old age of 90?
When Sarah was confronted about this, she lied;
She denied laughing, this denial is the same as a bold lie.
Jacob dressed like his brother Esau, to get Esau's blessing.
Saying I am Esau and I have fixed you some venison.
Jacob deceived his father Isaac on that day, he lied:
When you deceive someone for a cause, it's the same as lying.
Esau came home to get his blessing but found out he couldn't.
This brought a fight to where Jacob had to flee for his life.
Joseph was asked to find his brothers and their flocks.
The brothers threw Joseph into a well so he could be sold.
They told their father Jacob, that a lion killed his son.
Jacob was deceived, like deceived his father and brother.
No matter how you twist things around to sound like the truth.
The lie will be known, and that lie will come back to haunt you.

William T. Smith

DOG WALKING POET

I am starting to be called, "The dog walking poet".
I do not mind, even though they never bought a book.
One day they may end-up reading some of my poems.
When I become internationally known for my psalms.
When the work day is over, they may sit back and read.
They may understand that faith in God is what they need.
You cannot receive this unless you truly honestly repent.
That is; you must believe Jesus to this earth God has sent.
Not as a prophet, nor just to be a healer, but as God's Son.
Put these poems down, pick-up your Bible, he is the one.

William T. Smith

I SEE A DEER

As I was driving out through the country.
There was a scene that was pure luxury.
I looked out my window and seen a deer.
She was eating corn in a field that was near.
She looked up and seen where I was at.
She started to run and did not look back.
As I was going on down that country road.
There was a buck standing straight and bold.
I stopped and waited to see if he would move.
I tried to be silent and still, waiting for a mood.
But before I could get ,my camera for a picture.
He took off and quickly was out around the curve.

William T. Smith

ONE EYED JACK

I was once given a little dog, a pekingese dog.
He was mean, not friendly definitely not at all.
He was mistreated when young, and trusted no one.
Getting close to him was hard, but his trust I won.
There was only two of us that could walk with him.
Everyone else, he would send them a running.
Someone along the way punched out one of his eyes.
After that he liked no one and became very fierce.
My sister-in-law, Norma took to him with ease.
And Jack went with Norma, and they went bye bye.
I was told Jack was happy and lived a very good life.
She kept him away from people, and had no strife.
When he did die it was in the arms of my sister-in-law.
Who was very sad at his passing, so she bawled and bawled.
So please don't give up, no matter how you were mistreated.
There is someone that will love you, and give you peace.
That is what the Lord Jesus done for us, for we are sinners.
Jesus took our punishment and ready to give us a new home.
William T. Smith

PIT BULLS

I have two Pit Bulls named Johnny and June.
People say they are mean; they speak to soon.
Any child young or older, can play with them.
They will not try to hurt, because they are tame.
A dog will only do what they are trained for.
You train one to be mean— run for the door.
You train one to be good— you can let them run.
When children come to play— they will have fun.
It is the media that gives these dogs a bad reputation.
The media says: "Kill all of them before they attack".
I will tell you a truth, that the media will not.
It is not the dog, but the owner that should be shot.
When the owners start training these dogs properly.
Then the media will have to print a retraction.
Any animal trained right can be good; if not their bad.
It is up to the owner to make them friendly or not.
For a Pit Bull was not breed to be a frightful killer.
A Pit Bull was breed to be a protective nanny for children.

William T. Smith

IS LIFE WORTH LIVING

Is life really worth what we are living?
God created all of us as a triune being.
We are made from dirt and rock as it seems.
Look at the ingredients on a bottle of vitamins.
It's filled with all kinds of rocks and minerals.
Even our food comes from the ground and animals.
And with that the doctors say we are 90% water.
The dirt makes us solid, water brings it together.
I have been told, there is life in the water.
If you do not drink water, the body cannot work.
But what holds all of this together as we live?
It has to be the oxygen, or the air that we breathe.
So: is life really worth what we are living?
I say yes; There is a good reason for you to exist.
To be just dirt, water and oxygen is not enough.
We were created to be a thinking race, that is tough.
In order to live, we need Christ Jesus the Light in us.
Without Jesus, we are living but dead, just earthly dust.
With Jesus we have eternal life after this body decays.
Jesus is life, Jesus is bread, Jesus is Light, Jesus is God.

William T. Smith

WONDER TO BE

Ole Lord my God: You are a wonder to be.
You made 7 Billion people alike, but differently.
We are alike in many ways in this world.
But: very different when it comes to boy and girl.
In the way we think, as well as in the way we talk.
In the way we get things done that we have sought.
In what we like, as well as in the things we do.
Somewhat the same, but: differently for me and you.
We are different in the things we want or seek.
God has even given us all different fingerprints.
We say this is all done by a single cell or by chance.
If that is so, why is there so much chaos and confusion?
For I cannot see how one cell can create all of this.
I believe in a God that can create all that you can see.
The big bang is chaos, but: the universe has an order.
I believe in a creator God, that created this for sure.
Look around, everything has an order, it's all the same way.
You see this in every land, no matter where you stay.
Give the credit where the credit really is deserved.
To a creator God who created all you see in this universe.
Ole Lord God: You are a wonder to me in all this.
With all that I cannot see like Love- Happiness and Bliss.

William T. Smith

CHRISTMAS IS BEAUTIFUL

Christmas is a beautiful and very wonderful season.
Where we gather around and give thanks to our Savior.
There are those that does not believe in Jesus Christ.
But: they will decorate a tree with very beautiful lights.
And others that will drink themselves into a drunken blitz.
Wake-up the next morning, crying with their heads aches.
And those that likes all them sugar cookies to eat.
Never giving thanks to the one that furnished the treat.
Christmas is more than presents, drinking or even eating.
It is more than stores selling what others has created.
All of this may be fun and merry, but: not the reason.
But what makes this season so great; is Jesus, God's Son.
Jesus is the reason we have this great day of Christmas.
Jesus was born on this day, so our sin could be forgiven.
We celebrate the birth of Jesus; our Lord, King and Savior.
But: in reality, his death at the cross gives us God's favor.
We now know Jesus is Lord and King of all the earth, be still.
Praise him for he stood in the gap, was crucified on the hill.
So that you and I can have eternal peace this Christmas day.
You see Jesus arose, Jesus could not stay in that cold grave.

William T. Smith

MY PIT BULLS

My son went to a farm, received two Pit Bull dogs.
Are friendly and kind, but at best solid as a log.
I take them on a mile walk almost every day.
They are stout and tough, But: they do what I say.
When they snarl and bark, it sounds loud and fearsome.
One thing is for sure, they will protect not hurt a child.
A Pit Bull can be a very gentle dog, this I have found.
Their mind and body when trained right, is very sound.
A Pit Bull has the instinct to protect small children.
When you try to harm a child— they will attack.
For this is the reason the Pit Bull I truly want and like.
I know a child will be safe, they never will hurt or bite.

William T. Smith

GOD'S GIFT

God our Heavenly Father has given us a gift.
This gift is yours with no strings attached.
You cannot do anything, no nothing with this gift.
Until you reach out to the Father and accept it.
When you do this gift should be used everyday.
But a gift like this is really made to give away.
God our Father has given us this marvelous gift.
Here it is, this is the gift of salvation and peace.
You cannot have this gift until you reach out.
You take this gift from God, so it can be used.
The way you use this gift, is simply to give it away.
We do this by sharing your story to others day by day.
If you take this gift and hide it somewhere safe;
And you never really use it, it does you no good.
But: if you use this gift; then you will be happy.
For in using it brings Joy, Peace and Good Will.
Not just for you, but with everyone who sees it.
This Gift of Salvation is a very precious gift indeed.
It will last you a lifetime, even into God's eternity.
For when you give it away, we receive much more.
Now you should know Jesus is the Gift of Salvation.
The more you give Jesus away, the more he multiplies.
My prayer is that you will accept this Gift of Salvation.
And let Jesus keep you in happiness and be joyful.
For even in times of sorrow, Jesus is there to help.
That is a gift that everybody needs and to be shared.

William T. Smith

HOW TO BECOME A CHRISTIAN

By taking three steps, you can make the most important decision of your life— to accept Jesus as your personal Savior and Lord and His gift of forgiveness of your sins.

ADMIT

Admit to God that you are a sinner, Repent, turn away from your sin: For all have sinned, and come short of the glory of God; Roman 3:23. For the wages of sin is death; but the gift of God is eternal life through Jesus Christ our Lord. Romans 6:23.

Repent you therefore, and be converted, that your sins may be blotted out,, when the time of refreshing shall come from the presence of the Lord; Acts 3:19.

BELIEVE

By faith receive Jesus Christ as God's Son and accept Jesus' gift of forgiveness from sin. For God so loved the world, that he gave his only begotten Son, that whosoever believes in him should not perish, but have everlasting life. John 3:16. Jesus said unto him, I am the way, the truth, and the life; no man comes unto the Father, but by me. John 14:6. Neither is there salvation in any other: for there is none other name under heaven given among men, whereby we must be saved. Acts 4:12. But God commended his love toward us, in that, while we were yet sinners, Christ died for us. Romans 5:8. For by grace are you saved through faith; and that not of yourselves: it is the gift of God: Not of works, lest any man should boast. Ephesians 2:8-9. He came unto his own, and his own received him not. But as many as received him, to them gave he power to become the sons of God, even to them that believe on his name: Which were born, not of blood, nor of the will of the flesh, nor of the will of man, but of God. John 1:11-13.

CONFESS

Confess your faith in Jesus Christ as Savior and Lord. If we confess our sins, he is faithful and just to forgive us our sins, and to cleanse us from all unrighteousness.

I John 1:9. That if you shall confess with your mouth the Lord Jesus, and shall believe

in your heart that God raised him from the dead, you shall be saved. For with the heart man believes unto righteousness; and with the mouth confession is made unto salvation. For whosoever shall call upon the name of the Lord shall be saved. Romans 10:9-10&13.

If you choose right now to believe Jesus died for your sins and receive new life through Him, pray a prayer similar to the one that follows, as you call on Him alone, to be your Savior and Lord: But pray with an honest heart believing Jesus is your Savior, for He knows if you are sincere or not.

"Dear Heavenly Father, I know I am a sinner and have rebelled against You in many ways. I believe Jesus died for my sin that only through faith in His death and resurrection can I be forgiven. I now turn from my sin and ask Jesus to come into my life as my Savior and Lord. From this day forward, I will choose to follow Jesus. Thank You, Lord Jesus for loving me and forgiving me. In Jesus' name I pray. Amen".

After you have received Jesus Christ into your life, share your decision with another person. Following Christ's example, ask for baptism by immersion in your local church as a public expression of your faith. Therefore we are buried with him by baptism into death: that like as Christ was raised up from the dead by the glory of the Father, even so we also should walk in newness of life. Romans 6:4. As you have therefore received Christ Jesus the Lord, so walk you in him: Colossians 2:6